Broadcast
News Writing
for Professionals

Broadcast News Writing for Professionals

Jeff Rowe

Marion Street Press, Inc.
Oak Park, Illinois

Library of Congress Cataloging-in-Publication Data

pending

Cover illustration, top right, by Stacey Jordan

ISBN 0-9665176-2-8
Printed in U.S.A.
Printing 10 9 8 7 6 5 4 3 2 1

Marion Street Press, Inc.
PO Box 2249
Oak Park, IL 60303
866-443-7987
www.marionstreetpress.com

*Dedicated to my mom and dad,
who taught me the value of learning.*

Contents

Section 2: Writing

Introduction

Remember Hiroshima

Trust me, I'm a reporter. That line will earn you a few laughs at a party, but the reality is we do ask our fellow citizens to entrust us with a valuable role in society – information providers.

How important is that role?

Consider this. A few years ago, a television producer invited a survivor of the Hiroshima atomic bombing, Kazuo Yoshikawa of Tustin, Calif., to be an in-studio guest at a live half-hour television segment on the 50th anniversary of the inferno.

The 65-year-old survivor's command of English was a bit halting so the producer asked him if he would come in a half-hour early so the producer could go over the show's format and general line of questioning. You don't want a live in-studio guest to ask for questions to be repeated.

Yoshikawa agreed and presented himself promptly at the appointed time. The producer reviewed the basic questions that would be asked, and was satisfied the quiet-spoken man would be able to handle the interview.

But the producer had one more question.

I don't understand, he told the Hiroshima survivor. In the months before the dropping of the nuclear explosive, American forces had invaded Okinawa, captured Iwo Jima and charred Tokyo with firebombs. Didn't the Japanese people realize they were defeated? Why did they not pressure their leaders to surrender, thus avoiding the two atomic attacks?

The old man considered the question for a moment. "Many of us suspected we were not doing well," Yoshikawa said. "Too many airmen, sailors and soldiers were not returning and teenagers such as me were pressed into service working in factories."

Every journalist, and everyone who cherishes a free society, should remember what this man who had glimpsed into hell said next: "But our radio and newspapers told us we were winning."

Imagine how different things might have been on August 6, 1945 if Japan's news media had told the truth.

Telling the truth is our job but it's much more complicated than it might seem.

Our knowledge of the facts, concepts and ideas we are reporting and our command of the language must be at such a high level as to be worthy of the trust invested in us by our fellow citizens.

"Civilians" can mix up the difference between *imply* and *infer*; we must not.

In these ever-more-complex times, our language skills must be akin to a physician's knowledge of medicine or a pilot's knowledge of aviation. Carelessness by a doctor or pilot is not tolerated. Sloppy techniques are subject to rebuke. Mistakes are likely to harm.

Yet, the tool of our trade is a language that often seems to lack logic in its evolution.

How else can you explain why cars park on a driveway and drive on a parkway? Or why a hamburger is devoid of ham and a pineapple lacks both pine and apple. The plural of tooth is teeth so why is the plural of phone booth not phone beeth? A vegetarian eats vegetables; what does a humanitarian eat? Why do "slow down" and "slow up" mean the same thing? Why do overlook and oversee mean the opposite? How did apartments get that name when they are not apart but fastened together?

English reflects the creativity of its speakers and writers. Those of us who profess to use it professionally are obligated to develop our skills to a very high level. We have to like words the way a painter connects with colors, a musician with notes, and a dancer with steps.

I don't know why, but I want to find a way to get the words "fortnight" and "nomenclature" in news copy. I've never done so and can't imagine the occasion when I would not use "two weeks" instead of fortnight and "terms" instead of nomenclature. But it's the joy of discovery and the fulfillment in working with the words that brings satisfaction to the writer.

For most journalists, reporting is the more exciting of the journalist's twin duties – gathering the facts and writing the story. Movie producers know this; that's why they typically show reporters in the field but rarely at their desks. Such scenes would be rather dull. Hunched over the keyboard, the typical journalist types a burst of words, ponders them, backspaces a little, stares at the screen, inserts a phrase, shuffles through his or her notes, fidgets in the seat, sips some water and then – types another burst.

And yet the finished work can be as lyrical as a song, as evocative as a painting, and as rhythmic as a dance.

"Good writing may be magical, but it's not magic," says Chip Scanlan, director of the writing and reporting program at the Poynter Institute, a school for journalists in St. Petersburg, Florida. The tactics and strategies of good writing can be identified, analyzed and employed. That's what this book endeavors to do.

Precision is important. Some years ago, a network television affiliate reported that American Savings and Loan was in financial trouble. Worried depositors withdrew $40 million before the station corrected an error in its report. *North* American Savings and Loan was in trouble.

Recently, network evening news broadcast contained the following report, read by the anchor.

> "Remember the man who got fired after a female co-worker said he harassed her by discussing a certain Seinfeld episode? A judge has now thrown out a 25-million-dollar jury award the man won in court against his employer on grounds the man was about to be fired anyway."

That story drew a letter to the editor in *Shoptalk*, an electronic newsletter that focuses on broadcast news.

The letter writer said the network news item contained two factual errors: A judge did not overturn the verdict, a three-judge panel of Wisconsin's intermediate appellate court, the Wisconsin Court of Appeals, overturned the award. And the reason for overturning the award was not that the man was about to be fired anyway.

The letter was signed by Judge Ralph Adam Fine, one of the three judges on the appeals court panel that overturned the jury verdict. Judge Fine went on to write that as a guest lecturer at journalism classes at the University of Wisconsin-Milwaukee, he asked students how many of them ever had been involved in an incident that was reported in newspapers or television. The judge then asked how many thought the reports were accurate. Fewer than ten percent responded affirmatively.

Books have been written about perception and truth. All of us have heard family and friends describe the same event quite differently. Still, the problems in the network news report involved easily verifiable facts, and for those errors no excuse is sufficient.

Yet, even being factually correct is not good enough sometimes.

Writing coach John Sweeney notes that word choices can carry subtle but significant differences in meaning.

Consider for example, these two sentences:

"He steadfastly refused to compromise."

"He stubbornly refused to compromise."

Both sentences are colored by an adverb. "Steadfast" suggests adherence to principles; "stubborn" suggests rigid thinking. In a news report, where objectivity is our guide, the sentence would be best written without *steadfastly*, *stubbornly* or any other adverb. That's because a good writer focuses on selecting strong, but appropriate, verbs. The question of whether it is steadfast or stubborn can be left to commentators. Our role is that of a neutral observer.

Often, that is far more difficult than it may seem.

Take, for example, our choice of verbs in the sentence just discussed above. "Refused" connotes a sense of determination. Does that verb accurately describe the person and situation we are writing about? If we're not sure, then we are better off with a more neutral "declined."

Here's another simple example: "He said he was home the night of the robbery."

"Said" is neutral, imparting no hint that our subject may be lying.

Now suppose we change that verb and write: "He claimed he was home the night of the robbery."

We have injected doubt into his denial and we should be able to justify that choice of verbs by a sentence either before or after that gives the listener or viewer solid reason to question the denial.

Often what we observe and report is unpleasant. Some complain that the media bring them too much bad news, and we probably ought to work harder at injecting a few notes of hope into our work. Helping people find solutions is a legitimate element of journalism. We must tell people pollutants are killing fish in the stream, but a complete piece ought to include how experts say the contamination can be stopped.

In *News Values: Ideas for an Information Age*, Pulitzer Prize-winning journalist Jack Fuller writes that knowledge "is better served by journalists who accept a duty to tell the truth rather than to take an adversarial posture toward those in authority. The adversarial model encourages less than candor, which is why it is so subversive of good journalism. Furthermore, although journalists certainly participate in the marketplace of ideas, their role is not an advocate's. They review the debate and try to come up with some form of judgment. They act as surrogates who help the public discover and weigh the evidence. Their role should be more like the judge's than the lawyer's, more like the scholar's than the partisan's."

And a journalist's education never ends. "A lifetime is not enough for all the learning a writer needs," wrote Fuller. "As the message becomes more complicated, the challenge becomes greater. People are looking for more coherence, not less."

After taking over the *St. Louis Post* and the *Dispatch* in 1878, Joseph Pulitzer said "more crime, immorality and rascality is prevented by fear of exposure in newspapers than by all the laws – moral and statute – ever devised."

"Those who think the media should shield us from unpleasant people and ideas misunderstand the very role of the journalist," says Bob Steele of the Poynter Institute. "We may not like what we see and hear, but we benefit when we know more, not less."

What we do as journalists is vital to a free society and how effectively we communicate can mean the difference between life and death.

Just ask the Hiroshima survivor.

Section 1
Reporting

Chapter 1.1

News judgment and reporting

As you move out into the journalistic world, you will hear it said of some reporters, producers and editors that they have "good news judgment." But what is that?

How can the *New York Post* or Fox News trumpet stories that *The New York Times* or other network newscasts will not even mention? It's because each newspaper and station adopts its own news values. These may be spelled out in a statement of principles, but more often, these values are unwritten but still clearly understood. Or should be.

Those staffers deemed to have "good news judgment" typically have a keen understanding of the kinds of stories their station considers important. Those preferences are shaped by several considerations:

■ **Demographics and culture** – What is the age breakdown of the community? Racial composition? Principal industries? Core problems? Stories that might find a rapt audience in a town with many retirees might fall flat in a college town.

■ **Competition** – What sorts of stories do competing stations like to chase? How do newspapers serving the community treat the news? Where do radio stations in the city get their news? Does the television station have an alliance with a radio station or newspaper in the area? What about web sites that contain news of our town?

Monitoring all these news outlets is important. As people try to cram more and more work, chores and other activities into their day, the biggest obstacle for viewers, listeners and readers becomes time. We want to make sure people find our broadcast worthy of their time investment.

■ **Station values** – Often these are set by the general manager and news director and thus can, and do, change when new ones come along.

News judgment and reporting

The savvy reporter is a good student of all these factors, not as a tactic to cozy up to the bosses but because it makes sense not just to know your community thoroughly but also to know how your station covers it. Many journalists end up frustrated – or fired – because they failed to learn what is important to their news director.

As they make their way up the journalism ladder, producers and reporters tend to move around a good deal, especially in the early years of their careers. Most arrive in a new town knowing little beyond the locations of some neighborhoods where they might want to consider living. But with internet access to online versions of newspapers just a few clicks away, it's easier than ever to become familiar with the issues before you even arrive for day one of work at a new job. Smart journalists, ones who are committed to public service, make sure they do that.

The smart reporter understands the news director's values, priorities and style and learns to craft proposals that meet with those preferences. That's not to say you must devote yourself to pleasing the boss but rather to make sure your efforts fit into the big picture.

So how do you decide what is news?

The late David Brinkley once said, "News is what I say it is."

That sounds a bit pompous perhaps, but I think what Brinkley meant was that no absolute rules determine what makes a news story. What may seem like a terrific story idea to a reporter may be dismissed as drivel by the news director.

A well-thought-out news proposal is the foundation for a story that is well reported, which then is the framework for a story that is well written. It is those stories that have the greatest impact on viewers.

A news story typically has most if not all the following elements:

■ **Timeliness** – An event that happened this morning has a much better chance of making today's newscast than something that happened yesterday or last week – unless we can update the story.

■ **Proximity** – Did the event happen in our town? Our county? The truck that caught fire while loading at a factory on Main Street is much more important to our viewers than if the same incident happened at a town 50 miles away.

■ **Significance** – What are the implications of the event we are reporting? What will happen? If the answer to those questions is "not much," then perhaps we have a story with much flash but little power.

■ **Prominence** – Is the central figure in our story widely known? If the mayor is arrested for drunken driving, that's a big story. If a worker at a local factory is arrested on the same charge, it's unlikely to even make the newscast.

■ **Conflict** – Are two groups at odds over a proposal? Not every news story must have disagreement at its core, but a good percentage of news originates from disputes of one kind or another.

■ **Drama** – Many of the most memorable news stories contain a strong element of drama. The lawyer in a high-stakes case calls a surprise witness. A president fights to keep from being removed from office. A teacher tries to talk a student into turning in a gun.

■ **Interest** – A story can be lacking many of the above elements, but if viewers find it intriguing, that's often enough. Conversely, if we fail to make significant events interesting, then shame on us as journalists.

The best news stories have many, if not all the above elements. Do a checklist with your story proposal to see how it rates.

Hard news/soft news

Hard news refers to the events, accidents, announcements and developments that occurred today, and may still be under way. The challenge is to transform these happenings into stories with a beginning, middle and end – something more than a recitation of facts spiked with voices and a solemn stand-up.

The end of a breaking news event typically marks the beginning of the story.

The lead is the conclusion —— we say how much damage the storm caused, what the city council decided, and where the lightening struck and who was hurt.

Soft news, or features, are the stories that add flavor to the newscast but typically are not spun off daily developments. But they can be the most memorable to viewers.

If a train derails in town and one of the tanker cars explodes, that's hard news we have to tell today. But how a three-legged dog helps a woman in a wheelchair with her chores is a story we can tell tomorrow or next week.

News story parameters

Once you have honed in on a story idea though, some work remains before you start reporting. You must consider several factors before you begin reporting:

■ **Range** – What's the scope of your story? Will it require reporting from Bakersfield, Baltimore and Beirut, or just some B-roll from a local park and bites from people who play there?

■ **Dimensions** – What is the time frame for our story? Will we need archive tape?

■ **Approach** – Is the best way to tell our story by a profile, a round up, an update, a scene-setter or something else?

■ **Tone** – Is this a dispute, a tragedy, a comic incident? Setting the right mood is important.

■ **Theme** – Perhaps the most important element. What's our story about? Why are we asking for the viewers' attention? Some-where fairly high up in most news stories is a sentence that tells our audience: "Here's why I am telling you this."

References

Thanks to easy computer access to mountains of knowledge, every reporter should be able to begin field reporting and interviewing knowing at least something about the subject. Learn how to find information on the internet and how to use various databases to research your topic.

Consider the following example of the power of information to a reporter:

Through police scanners, reporters at the station learned of a gunman holding several hostages in a commercial building nearby. The station quickly notified reporters at their partner newspaper and reporters from both organizations soon were on the scene. There, police told reporters they believed the gunman had arrived in a pick-up truck parked in front of the building.

Reporters called in the truck's license number to the newspaper's library, where a researcher ran the plate number through the Department of Motor Vehicles database. That produced a name and address. Within minutes, reporters in the newsroom using a telephone directory that lists phone numbers by address had found names and telephone numbers of the gunman's neighbors and were interviewing them on the phone.

Meanwhile, another researcher was checking voter registration, property records, and various news databases for other information on the sus-

Newsroom organization

A broadcast news organization is structured differently than a newspaper because it operates in a fundamentally different way.

Reporters on a newspaper staff are expected to be in command of their beats; to know what is happening and when, and to be able to make recommendations for coverage to their editor. An education reporter, for example, might talk to his or her editor on Monday morning about the week ahead. The reporter would outline a plan for the week – research a proposed story on bilingual education on Monday, cover the school board meeting Tuesday evening, write an explanatory feature on Wednesday based on a decision anticipated at the school board meeting, more research on the bilingual enterprise story on Thursday, write the story on Friday. On a newspaper, the editors typically are coaches rather than assigners. The reporter brings the agenda to the editor.

It works almost the opposite way in television.

Radio and television reporters almost never can plan their week. A typical television station might employ a fifth of the news staff of a daily newspaper in the same area and so it must deploy its resources much differently. After an early meeting with the news director and executive producer, the assignment editor typically decides which reporters and photographers will cover what stories.

Television reporters usually have more latitude over what they cover for morning broadcasts, which have grown so enormously in scope in recent years that the number of viewers equals or exceeds evening newscasts. No longer are the evening newscasts the "electronic hearth" they used to be, with the family gathered after work and school to see what happened in the world.

pected hostage-taker.

By the time the gunman surrendered peacefully an hour later, the paper and station had confirmed his identity and assembled a profile.

Learn how to use all the tools available to you as a reporter; the information you gather will enrich your writing.

Some journalists are better reporters than writers; that is, they are better at gathering the facts than assembling them into a smooth script. But the baseball player who is a better fielder than hitter cannot simply surrender at the plate. Dedicated athletes, and dedicated journalists, work on their weaknesses.

In radio, "morning drive," the hours people are commuting to work and often listening to the radio, is the day's biggest radio audience. Perhaps those same listeners are too frazzled going home from work to listen.

In radio and television, the news director usually has the final call as to what goes on air. His or her job is equivalent to the top editor at a newspaper.

Here's a brief description of the various jobs in a television newsroom. Radio operates in similar fashion but lacks all the people who deal with pictures.

■ **News director** – Decides the general tone and thrust of a station's coverage.

■ **Producer** – Assembles the newscast, often doing much of the writing.

■ **Assignment editor** – Decides what reporters and photographers will cover.

■ **Reporter** – Gathers information and bites on assigned stories. In small stations, reporter also may photograph his/her own stories and also may edit them.

■ **Editor** – Puts together the news packages, working from the script written by the reporter and tape shot by the photographer.

■ **Graphic artist** – Creates graphics and other on-screen artwork as needed by the newscast.

■ **Engineer** – Responsible for keeping everything running.

■ **Researcher/librarian** – Larger stations may have a specialist who can help producers and reporters find information needed for a story.

Covering beats

At larger newspapers, reporters develop specialties; they become experts in a certain topic area – aviation, agribusiness, the economy, politics, tourism, etc.

Newspapers can do that because — depending on advertising sales – they simply can add pages for more news. But radio and television are linear – that is, they only can broadcast one story at a time, no matter how big the station. That explains why a television station's news staff is smaller than the staff of the newspaper in the same town. Given the smaller staff, television news reporters rarely can count on working a beat in the same way their print counterparts can.

Broadcast journalists therefore must learn a little about a lot because they often will find themselves covering wildly different stories in the course of a single day, particularly at small stations. They may cover a bank robbery in the morning, a business outlook conference in the afternoon, and a school board meeting in the evening. (It can be a long work day in a small town.)

One beat all broadcast reporters should be able to cover is politics.

Some say the tools, techniques and tricks political operatives bring to an election have outpaced the media's knowledge in dealing with them. These campaign managers know, for example, that media scrutiny for a state or national candidate in a small or medium-sized city likely will be far less than the scrutiny in a major metropolitan area. Campaign managers know that the smaller the town, the more likely the tenor of coverage will be uncritical, if not giddy and adoring. They know reporters in smaller cities tend to be less experienced and often will settle for rehearsed bites from the candidate.

We can do better. Here are some tips drawn from dozens of journalists and compiled by *Editor & Publisher* magazine:

Go easy on the polls. Yes, it's useful information – if we explain how the candidates are adjusting their campaign and how the polls signal shifts in public thinking. But too often, polling information is presented as a score, as if the election were a game.

Speak to real people, who often have very different priorities than the ones candidates are talking about. At a recent municipal election in California, the media focused almost exclusively on the candidates' attacks on each other. But at a candidate's forum, all of the questions were about traffic, growth and safety.

Resist bombarding listeners and viewers with peripheral information. How many houses a candidate owns is important, but if our audience knows more about the candidate's various residences than the how the candidate's health plan will work, then we probably ought to shift our focus a bit.

Look into the backgrounds of candidates. Treat them as applicants for a job. Talk to past and present employers, colleagues, neighbors, customers, suppliers – anyone and everyone who comes into significant contact with the candidate. How well they campaign is important but what we really want to present to our listeners and viewers is sufficient information to allow them to judge how well the candidate will govern. That may mean we have to raise questions the candidates are avoiding.

Press beyond the stereotypes. This can be difficult because the media herd can cling to collective beliefs about a candidate. Be strong enough to explore beyond the accepted version of a candidate's strengths and weaknesses.

Be a relentless fact checker. Make sure we carefully check candidate's statements and ensure that we inform our audience about any variations in the truth.

Chapter 1.2

Finding memorable stories

Much of our time as reporters is consumed doing the stories we must – fires, crime, natural calamities, conflicts of one kind or another, the machinations of governments, people, places and events that have been thrust into the news. Good reporters learn how to do all those stories well.

Great reporters go beyond that. They not only get steadily better at their assigned work, but they also manage to find time and resources to report stories that go beyond the swirl of events that clamor for attention. It's these enterprise stories that tend to be the most engaging for us as reporters.

In the course of your career, you often will hear news directors and speakers at journalism conferences say, "Good reporting leads to good writing." That's true. But a step is missing. A good *idea* inspires good reporting, which then nourishes good writing.

Reporters who consistently come up with memorable enterprise story ideas are prized, and viewers remember their work because it gives meaning and wider understanding to their lives.

Perhaps the worst dismissal former *Wall Street Journal* deputy editor Barney Calame makes is to say a story offers little more than a "great command of the obvious." The work of disciplined reporters rarely falls into that category – they have developed a system of generating good enterprise pieces and memorable stories that surprise, delight and enrich.

Charles Kuralt of CBS News made a career telling memorable stories. Among his classics were how a self-educated man in rural Arkansas built a library; and why a North Carolina man kept a fleet of bicycles for poor neighborhood children to use. No assignment editor sent him on those stories – he found them.

Finding memorable stories

Finding memorable enterprise stories requires the development of good newsgathering habits:

■ Read widely: Newspapers, magazines, books.

Be alert for causes and effects. For example, many people don't like to fly small airplanes, so many regional airlines have been switching to bigger aircraft. Had you been the first to notice that trend, you would have had a terrific story.

Look for interesting people. In the course of reporting a story on oil leases years ago, I met a man who had worked in the "awl bidnis" for 75 years. Right away, I knew he was someone upon whom I could center a memorable story on changes in the industry. Moreover, I also had obtained another source for covering the oil industry.

Be on the lookout for connections. In every story, ask, "What happens next?" A journalist has, in effect, a license to wonder and then ask people for answers.

Explore the contrarian path. Riding a car, train or bus to work is normal; if you find someone who roller-skates to work, you may have a story.

Memorable stories connect with the viewer emotionally. As ace Fox News reporter Chris Blatchford says: "For a story to be powerful, the viewer has to feel something when it is finished."

Elements of a good enterprise story

A good enterprise story tends to have all, or at least most, of the following elements:

Engaging lead
Strong focus and theme
Something unexpected, surprising
Vivid characters
Natural sound breaks
Perspective – A window on something not opened before
■ Powerful close that gives viewers a sense of completion

Here are some tips to consistently develop good story ideas:

Know a little about an ever-widening range of topics. Business. Weather. What a city manager's responsibilities are. How the National Transportation Safety Bureau works. A basic familiarity with our institutions and how they work will help you recognize when something is amiss.

Become an expert in a least one reporting area – politics, education, health, transportation, business or some other topic that interests you.

Read the newspaper in your town thoroughly, and trade magazines and newsletters that relate to your coverage area. For example, if you cover city government, find out what professional publications the city manager reads. Many of these publications will put reporters on their mailing lists free. It's a great way to stay tuned to issues facing your beat.

Monitor relevant web sites.

Be alert for good stories everywhere. That doesn't mean you should carry a notebook and video camera to a party, but I've lost track of how many stories have originated in a comment at a social gathering. People are relaxed and talkative and we as reporters are really professional listeners.

Decide where your story fits into the normal news progression – breaking news, follow-up feature, or enterprise.

Effectively covering your beat

■ Always ask your sources and interview subjects "what's new?" and at the conclusion of the interview: "Anything else we have not covered?"

Every story has a life

Many stories are isolated incidents that we report before moving on to the next incident. Other stories clearly must be updated throughout the day – a fire at a nursing home, the search for a missing child, a standoff between police and a hostage-taker. These are the easy ones to update because typically new information becomes available as events progress.

Sometimes though, we have to work hard to update or freshen a story. We have to do some reporting to figure out what might happen next.

For example, if at 6 p.m. you are reporting that the mayor is proposing an ordinance that would impose fines on teens caught smoking, make sure you freshen your report for the 11 p.m. newscast to include what the next steps are, what the reaction is, and what the proposal's chances are of passage.

Far too many stories slip silently beneath the waves of the next day's events. You can distinguish yourself as a reporter by following up on people and events that have been in the news. What happened to the man we reported was arrested last week? Six months later, had the workers who lost their jobs in the takeover battle found new work? What about the woman who lost everything she owned when her apartment building collapsed in flames?

If you did the original story well, your audience also will enjoy the follow-up.

When out reporting, strive to come back with more story ideas.

Never give up on a story idea that makes sense.

Look for commonality in events.

Anticipate what could happen.

Look beyond the obvious for causes, driving forces, the future.

Think in two directions – Look for ways to localize national or global events and trends; and nationalize, or relate local events to the bigger picture.

■ Consider time references – past, present and future.

■ Consider scope – how far should you stray from your central point.

Consider the constituencies – who is affected.

■ Keep a file of people and events to revisit later.

Keep a good source list. Use it. Update it. Add to it daily.

Next steps include:

■ Do a database search. That will help refine your idea and also will help you avoid a story that has "a great command of the obvious."

Decide on the focus – narrow is usually better than wide.

Decide on the tone – amusing, angry, heart tugging.

■ Decide on a tactical approach – single profile, collective, round up. Be sure to check profiles thoroughly. For a reporter, about as bad as it gets is to learn after a sympathetic profile airs that our subject isn't quite the victim or angel we represented him or her to be in our piece.

Now it's time to write a proposal for our news director, assignment editor or producer. A two-or-three-paragraph summary is fine. Make sure though, that it contains a sentence that begins, "This is important, significant, interesting because..."

Few reporters bother to go through these steps. Instead they approach

Localizing/nationalizing

It's important to connect stories to our viewers and listeners, and a good reporter looks for ways to do that in every story. That means putting stories in context – is the phenomenon we are reporting confined to our area alone? Do the extra bit of reporting it takes to be able to authoritatively tell viewers that the fire ant infestation in our area also is a problem in other parts of the nation.

Conversely, the smart reporter will follow news of the nation and world with keen interest. Why? Because the enterprising reporter will find links from some of these far-flung events to local interests, which can help us bring national and global developments home.

For example, the factional fighting in Kosovo seems beyond the direct concern of most Americans. But what if we find a group of Albanian immigrants in our area? Their views and reactions to the fighting, and interactions with their homeland, might make for a compelling story.

A local soldier returned from peacekeeping duty in some faraway land could be a source for a story relating the difficulty of the mission.

In both cases, listeners and viewers will be able to relate to one person or one family's experience much easier than to all the stories about masses of refugees or a detachment of troops. It's the way we are as humans – we connect with each other one at a time.

the assignment editor between telephone calls and say "how about if we do something on... " The editor may nod and the reporter may then feel victorious. "I'm doing the story I wanted to do!"

But it is unlikely to be nearly as strong a package as it could have been had the reporter done enough research first to be able to offer a story thesis. Be a professional in every way.

Once you have approval to pursue the project, you must remain disciplined and focused. An outline becomes critical. Unlike work on a daily story – where we write the piece all in one sitting after the reporting is finished – it's helpful in a larger story to begin writing at the start of the reporting process. That will help us see where the holes are – where we need to do more reporting, what additional pictures we need.

The bigger the package, the more important it is to keep it moving briskly. We can employ the "gold coins along the trail technique" – offering the viewers nuggets along the way reinforce and sustain interest. For more writing techniques, see Chapter 2.2

Chapter 1.3

Interviewing tactics and techniques

Drawing people out – getting them to speak from the heart – is one of the journalist's most challenging tasks. Interviewing is both an art and a science.

Good interviewers get better material because they are able to put the people they interview at ease, establish a rapport, and win their trust. They do this by showing a genuine interest in what the person they are interviewing has to say, focusing on being a better listener than a talker, and remaining alert for information to pursue.

Demonstrate an interest in your interviewee by asking some get-acquainted questions before plunging into the interview. Without being a spy, look for obvious things about the person that you can inquire about. Is that a Harley-Davidson in your garage? Did I read correctly that you once were an Air Force nurse? Does that Oriole logo on the wall mean you are a Baltimore fan? Such questions not only help your subject relax for the interview, but also may reveal clues about motivation and personal history.

That's the "art" of the interview.

The "science" part of interviewing is an acquired skill. Know the basics and you will, much more often than not, come away with a successful interview. What we want is for the people we are interviewing to open up beyond a "yes/no interview" and technical explanation of a topic – we want our interview subjects to reveal their motivations, hopes, dreams and fears.

Here are some tips for getting a good interview:

Prepare. With vast amounts of information on the internet and on various databases, it's easier than ever before to gather a dossier of information on a subject. Double check your facts and figures.

A five-person staff gathers information for Tim Russert of *Meet the Press* so he is thoroughly prepared for interviews. A *Washington Post* piece on Russert said his "prosecutorial approach –'you said this in 1991, let's put it on the screen' – turns each interview into a deposition."

Russert said he developed the technique because "it became so tiresome having these trivial discussions where the guest says 'I didn't say that' or 'you took it out of context.' I said 'let's end all that – put it on the screen.' "

Most broadcast journalists consider themselves lucky if they work in a place with one researcher. Still, in the electronic age, we have little excuse for not researching interview subjects thoroughly.

Plan. The people we interview typically fall into one of several categories: the executive or leader, mid-level manager, line worker, official spokesperson, witness, victim, accused or hostile participant. The information and perspective available from people in each of these groups is vastly different. Know what information you want – and can get – from each. For example, the line worker – the ordinary working bloke – likely will have a keen perspective on how a project is working in the field. But that same worker may be a poor source on the broad company objectives.

Brief the subject. With its array of lights, microphones, cameras and other equipment, television newsgathering can be intimidating, especially to those who are undergoing their first encounter with the electronic beast. Take time to explain what the equipment does. Engage your subject in conversation before the formal interview begins and it will be much easier to shift into the real thing.

Develop an interviewing style that fits you. Sam Donaldson blusters and scolds. Diane Sawyer is a blend of an older protecting sister and probing aunt. Rather than copying someone else's approach, develop techniques that work for you.

Build up to the tough questions.

Probe for answers beyond clichés. People's motivations often are complex. They may indeed have been driven to report their company's practice of dumping toxic chemicals because of their concern for the environment, but were they also at least partially motivated by the reward? They may not tell us that directly, but if we ask what they plan to do with the money we certainly will get a clue.

Avoid questions that can be answered with a yes or no. Also, avoid complex or multiple-part questions. Short questions are best. Why did you do that? How did this happen?

Use silence to your advantage, especially when asking a tough question. The subject may say, "I don't want to talk about that." Say nothing for a few moments – you will be amazed at how many people are uncomfortable with silence and will rush to fill it with an explanation that moments ago they said they would not give.

Realize that it's a natural human tendency to coach – to explain what you know. Most people thoroughly enjoy being cast as an expert. Take advantage of that desire: Ask people to simplify. Never go away until you comprehend the answer. Preface a question with "Can you help me understand... ." Be like Colombo, a police investigator played by Peter Falk years ago in a television series. He played dumb – forever asking people to explain things. They did, and he solved the case every week.

Minimize your own role. We're listeners; the people we are interviewing are the talkers.

Avoid responding verbally or with head nods to your subject's answers. The "um's" and "I see's" will be picked up by the microphone, marring the interview tape. And on tape, head nods will look like agreement, which is an image we do not want to convey. As journalists, we're neutral observers.

Have an alternative plan if everything you plan goes wrong.

Difficult interviews

If the interview is likely to be a difficult or even hostile one, be prepared.

Ask simple, specific questions rather than complex ones. For example, asking a suspected mafia figure if he is engaged in organized crime is likely to produce a "no" answer. To the mafia chieftain, what he operates is a "business." A better questioning strategy would be to inquire, "How do you earn your money?"

Avoid questions that are so open-ended that they are the equivalent of handing over the microphone to the subject with instructions to "say whatever you want." For example, a question that begins "what can you tell us about... " gives the subject a free pass to make completely self-serving statements. Such questions also signal to our interview subject that our knowledge of the subject is skimpy.

Be careful not to load qualifiers onto your questions. Your interview subject may truthfully answer "no" to the question: "Did you embezzle money from the Amalgamated Textile trust fund?" A better question would be: "Have you ever stolen anything from anyone?"

Strive to get your subject to reveal basic facts. To do this, avoid words and phrases that automatically assign guilt. For example, asking a Serbian Army officer if his troops committed genocide almost certainly will produce a "no" response. To the Serbs, the Albanians were the enemy. Much better for the journalist to ask: "Why were unarmed civilian Albanians

31

killed?"

Silence can be especially effective when interviewing politicians and others who have been coached to stick to the message they want to deliver. Often, the first answer the reporter hears will be the crafted one. If the reporter is disciplined enough to let a few seconds of silence hang, the interviewee often will continue with an explanation. Sometimes a little more silence will elicit the emotional, from-the-heart response we want.

Interviewing the FBI way

Journalists and agents of the Federal Bureau of Investigation have much in common. Journalists and FBI agents both research a subject before going out on interviews. Journalists and FBI agents both want truthful information from interviews.

It gets a little different after that; a journalist goes back to the office, studio or live truck to write a story; the FBI agent may handcuff the interview subject and cart him or her off to jail. But an FBI agent typically knows far more about the art and science of interviewing than the typical reporter, because he has honed successful tactics and techniques over decades of work.

FBI Special Agent Joseph Stuart specialized in interviewing and taught other agents how to conduct successful ones. In his classes, Stuart immediately distinguishes between an interview, which he calls a "conversation with a purpose," and an interrogation, which he defines as "a confession against self interest."

In television police dramas, the antagonist often blurts out the truth in the closing minutes, just in time for a brief, happy closing scene that fades to the commercial break. In reality, such confessions come rarely. Rather, Stuart teaches, the interview subject usually reveals the truth in small bits, one piece building on another. It's up to the interviewer to build rapport with the interview subject. Questions asked in an accusing tone are less likely to induce the interviewee to speak than questions phrased in more neutral tones.

The first step in a successful interview is to study the case, if you are an FBI agent; the background of the story, if you are a journalist.

The next step is to determine the best place for the interview. People tend to be most comfortable in familiar surroundings, Stuart says. Second choice is a neutral setting; third choice is the office of the interviewer. Wherever the site, Stuart says it's important that it be private, quiet, and free of interruptions.

Good journalists prepare a list of questions or talking points, but Stuart says the answers are just one part of what a person being interviewed reveals – if we know what to observe. Just seven percent of communication is verbal content, Stuart says. Thirty-eight percent is vocal – how the interviewee speaks – and 55 percent is visual. (See more on this below.)

Bizarro By Dan Piraro

One question, Mr. President! — This is our first trip to Washington. Will you take our picture together in front of the Capitol?

© Dan Piraro. Reprinted with special permission of King Features Syndicate

Television interviews can be particularly unnerving for interviewees, particularly the first time. The lights, a big camera on a tripod, and the presence of another person – the photographer – can make it very difficult to put the interviewee at ease.

Stuart tells agents he trains that their introduction can set the tone for the entire interview. He suggests the straightforward approach works best – introduce yourself, tell what you do, where you work, and what you want.

That last element is critical because it is the first step in rapport building, which Stuart defines as the "establishment of non-threatening common ground between the interviewer and the interviewee."

Here's Stuart's "rapport checklist":

Put the subject at ease. Ask questions about his or her job, his or her family, his or her hobbies.

Address his concerns. A kidnapping suspect once began an interview with Stuart by saying "I don't want to go to prison." Stuart countered with "right now, my concern is getting that little girl back. Let's do that first." The tactic worked.

Encourage her to talk. Be an attentive, interested listener.

Communicate that you are human, too. Be flexible and willing to let the interview digress a little.

To keep rapport alive, Stuart recommends:

■ Don't give unsolicited advice.

■ Don't downgrade the other person's status.

■ Don't interrupt.

■ Don't finish sentences for the interviewee.

■ Don't change the subject.

■ Don't tell them their concerns are groundless.

■ Don't do something else while they talk.

In questioning, FBI agents are taught to begin with open-ended questions and build to more specific ones. That works well for journalists too.

FBI agents also are taught to close interviews by asking "catch-all" questions:

■ Is there anything else I should be aware of?

■ Is there anything I forgot to ask?

■ Is there anything else you want to tell me?

Sometimes those questions elicit the best information of all.

Determining if your interview subject is being truthful

Every day, juries in court try to determine if someone is telling the truth. As journalists, we cannot achieve the same finality of determination as a court. So we must learn to observe signals given by our interview subjects as they respond to our questions. Here are some telltale signs developed by the FBI to determine if a person is being truthful or lying:

Behavioral signs

The truthful person:

■ Sits upright but not rigid.

■ Positions himself/herself in front of the questioner.

■ Leans toward the questioner when making a point.

■ Appears relaxed and casual.

The deceptive person:

■ Slouches or leans back in the chair or sits unnaturally stiff in the chair.

■ Positions himself/herself to the side of the questioner, rather than in front.

■ Pulls elbows in close, folds arms in front, crosses legs.

■ Exhibits rapid and erratic posture changes.

Verbal signals

The truthful person:

■ Makes general, sweeping denials.

■ Offers unqualified, direct, and spontaneous answers.

■ Exhibits a reasonable memory.
■ Responds to questions rationally in a distinct and clear tone of voice.

The deceptive person:
■ Offers very specific denials.
■ Gives delayed, evasive, or vague answers.
■ Exhibits an unusually poor, selective or remarkable memory.
■ Speaks in an irrational, mumbled or subdued manner, using fragmented sentences.

Consider this transcript of part of Connie Chung's interview with Congressman Gary Condit in August 2001, several months after Chandra Levy disappeared. Levy was an intern in his office; Condit had acknowledged to police that she was a "close friend."

Chung: Was it a sexual relationship?

Condit: Well, Connie. I've been married for 34 years, and, uh, I've not been a... perfect man, and I've made my share of mistakes. But um, out of respect for my family, and out of a specific request from the Levy family, I think it's best that I not get into those details uh, about Chandra Levy.

Chung: Did you at any time ask the staff to lie?

Condit: I flew my wife to Washington.

Chung: Did you at any time ask your staff to lie?

Condit: Well let me, let me finish this. Let me finish this. Let me finish this. Because you're making the accusation. I think it's a very important one. That I have not been cooperative. And I'm puzzled by why the police chief would say that. I don't think there's anyone in Washington D.C. who's been more cooperative in this investigation than myself. And I'm confused by why the police chief would say that. Several weeks before that, the chief and...

Was Condit being truthful? Perhaps, but in just a few sentences he exhibited none of the verbal practices of a truthful person and all of the verbal manifestations of a deceptive one. The smart reporter would ask questions that a small step at a time would induce Condit to reveal the nature of his relationship with Levy. But Chung did not have enough time, one of the dilemmas of live broadcasts.

Figuring out if someone is being truthful has been a challenge for journalists since the first newspaper. Knowing the behavior characteristics of truthful people and liars will help a skilled reporter frame follow-up questions.

In asking those questions, remember this tip from FBI polygraph expert Tony Caruso: Guilty people rarely blurt out a confession the way they sometimes do on television dramas. But the skilled questioner can elicit step-by-step acknowledgments that will lead to the same conclusion.

Interviewing the media savvy

Increasingly, government officials, business leaders and sports figures respond to interview questions so smoothly and with such precise answers that it seems as if they have been coached.

They have.

Politicians, executives and athletes often are tutored by experts on how to handle the media. They learn how to appear cool and confident on camera, how to shape their responses to include the points they want to make, and how to parry tough questions.

It can be extremely frustrating for a journalist to interview the media savvy – unless the journalist knows how to fashion questions to penetrate the interviewee's defenses.

John Sawatsky is a Canadian reporter and author who has developed some acclaimed techniques for getting the media savvy to open up. He recommends, among other things, asking short, open-ended questions. Yes, these often will produce practiced responses, but then the reporter can ask for evidence and examples to support the source's assertion. Sawatsky also recommends putting the burden of proof on the source. If the interviewee says no crime was committed, ask "how do you know that?"

Avoid the long, multi-part questions reporters often are seen and heard asking at presidential news conferences, Sawatsky says, because the media-wise interviewee will focus only on the segment of the multi-part interrogatory that he or she can best answer.

Reporters also should avoid trying to highlight their own personalities in interviews, Sawatsky says. Television reporters do this all the time. We see cutaway shots of them nodding, fluttering their eyelids, or otherwise preening for the camera.

In seminars, Sawatsky shows a tape of CBS anchorman Dan Rather's interview with Mirjana Markovic, the wife of Yugoslav President Slobodan Milosevic. In the interview, Rather tried to get Markovic to admit to ethnic cleansing and other atrocities in Yugoslavia. But Markovic never lost control of the interview. She denied Rather's assertions, blamed the United States, and resolutely defended her husband's role as one of statesmanship and fighting off terrorists. In Sawatsky's view, Rather blew it.

Instead of asking short, open-ended questions and specific queries about specific incidents, he asked closed-end ones, such as "When will you stop killing Kosovar Albanians?" That question failed to force Markovic to either agree to a general fact or offer evidence to the contrary. A better line of questioning might have been to ask about a specific instance of genocide or the open-ended: "What will it take to stop the fighting?"

Although you may use Sawatsky's tactics faithfully, some interviewees are so guarded, focused and prepared that it is impossible to draw them out.

Some years ago, I interviewed a congressman for a half-hour on a television news program. I had my questions carefully planned and I paid attention to the answers, alert for something to pursue that was not on my list of topics. I was unable to find one. I feared the best that viewers could draw from my efforts was a conclusion that the congressman was in favor of goodness and against evil.

Reporting and writing profiles

Sometimes, the interview is the story. If we can persuade someone who has been in the news to consent to an interview, we have a story, especially if we are the first.

Now the challenging part begins – preparing to do that profile.

Most people will speak on a surface level – telling us their positions on this issue or that, confirming high points of their biography, and maybe parting with a "safe" dream or goal. But profiles based on such information often read like a narrative resume. We can do better.

We may not get our interview subjects to reveal their most closely held hopes and fears but we can ask questions designed to give listeners, viewers and readers a revealing portrait of our subject.

Barbara Walters is famous for winning the confidence of her interview subjects and inducing them to share their thoughts and feelings.

She does this by making good use of one question – Why? Why did you do that? Why did you go there? Why do you say that?

In creating a profile of someone, here are some questions that can help our interview subjects relax and provide some intriguing information. Moreover, the answers to these questions can lead us to many follow-up "why" questions.

What was your first job and what did you learn?

What was your proudest accomplishment?

Who is your personal hero?

What are your hobbies?

What recent movie would you recommend?

What recent book would you recommend?

People in high school said you were...

What adjectives would you use to describe yourself?

A great day off or evening for you would be...

What is your best childhood memory?

What are the most important lessons you learned from your mother and father?

What is your most treasured possession?

What was your most humbling experience?

Do you have any regrets?

What is most important to you in life?

What is your favorite car?

What are your favorite web sites?

Only your family and closest friends know that you're...

If you were president you would...

After work you like to...

What advice you would give to students aspiring to a career in your field?

You are really happy when...

What three famous people would you like to join for supper and conversation?

Interviewing the grieving

High on most reporters' list of assignments to avoid is interviewing the grieving. Knocking on the door of a family who has just experienced tragedy seems intrusive; sticking a microphone in the face of a parent who has just lost a child seems cruel. But often we must seek these people out because what has happened is news. How we approach them is critical, not just because it will determine what information we get, but because we want to be considerate, good citizens.

So knock on the door and tell whomever answers who you are and that you want to help people remember the deceased. Sometimes, people will say no, preferring to grieve privately. We want to respect that. But often, family and friends want to help others remember a lost one. A year after a teenager died on an outing in the desert, his father told me why he had spent time with me the day after his son's death. Even as he was engulfed in a shroud of grief, he said he nonetheless realized that if he told me the story of his son's death, he would not have to go though the emotional gauntlet of retelling it again and again. He would simply show people our report. And that's what he did.

Psychologists say it can be therapeutic to talk about great emotional trauma. If we're courteous, we can knock on the door of the grieving without guilt. And when we're invited inside to share recollections of someone's life, we should remember that seemingly small details in life often are more revealing than grander, more public elements of personality.

After the September 11 tragedy in New York, *The New York Times* profiled every one of the 2,000-plus victims of the twin towers attacks. Most of the profiles ran five or six paragraphs – about the length of a typical 90-second television news story. Short as they were, the profiles nonetheless often were tremendously revealing and emotionally powerful portraits of each of the victims, even though they lacked many of the usual biographical touchstones – high school graduation date, sports played, memberships in civic groups.

Consider these profiles and think about what they tell about the person:

Alison Wildman: She had just met a nice man. And the results of her test for a certified financial analyst's license had arrived – although she had not yet garnered the strength to look at them. After Ms. Wildman's death, her sister opened the envelope. She had passed.

Vincent Slavin: "Once, a co-worker mentioned in conversation that she would love to see the Oscars in person. Just like that, he got her tickets. He used to introduce me as his brother from another mother. I was proud of that."

Edward Schunk: His wife says that he must be in heaven. "I know he's waiting for me until we meet again," she said.

Tara McCloud-Gray: "She was a precise person with everything in its place," her mother said. "She was a no-nonsense girl. I know she is gone but there are times I have picked up the phone and dialed her number."

Andrew Rosenblum: "There was something magical about my brother," said Adam Rosenblum, the youngest of Andrew's three siblings. "All I ever wanted was to be just like him."

Eugene Whelen: He kept extra winter jackets in his jeep in

case he spotted a shivering, homeless person. During a school visit (to the firehouse where he worked), he asked why one child was left on the bus. The child was paralyzed, the teacher replied. Mr. Whelen carried the child to the fire truck.

Christopher Ingrassia: At a recent business dinner with several of his bosses and several clients, he could not help but overhear the argument between the man and woman at the table behind them. The man then got up, threw a napkin in the woman's face and left the restaurant. Chris turned around said, "Don't worry about it; you're with us now."

In reporting our profile, it's important to be thorough.

That means speaking to relatives, friends, colleagues and anyone who knew the person. A treasure trove of information often is available online, including voter information, business filings and prison records. If appropriate, we also might need to search through court filings – federal, tax, state, bankruptcy and divorce.

We always should complete a basic Nexis or other news database search. We would look foolish and certainly poorly serve our audience if we broadcast an adoring piece about a coach, for example, only to have a viewer produce a news report from years ago about the coach beating up some fans.

Look for themes in people's lives, but know that most people are more complex and nuanced than they often are portrayed in the media.

Be a mental vacuum for telling details that reveal patterns, beliefs and values. For example, the winged pig hanging from the ceiling of the lawyer's office is probably much more revealing about his state of mind than the framed law degree on the wall.

Be a professional – always

Maintain your self-respect – and treat everyone with respect. No interview is worth groveling and begging.

When the Unabomber, Ted Kaczynski, was arrested, the network media stars practically tripped over themselves in a rush to get Kaczynski to agree to an interview. The media newsletter *Shoptalk* (www.shoptalk.com) obtained some of the letters network producers and correspondents sent the Unabomber. Some of these letters are embarrassing; others are *very* embarrassing.

Here are excerpts from some of the letters:

"I was born not far from where you now live and have a cabin in the woods west of Colorado Springs that has no electricity or running water."

You will have a "chance to explain your experiences to our huge audience and also the opportunity to share your views and concerns, which I know you have long wanted to do."

"This interview would help to bring more readers to your book and better understanding of your legal appeal."

"Our story will allow you to personally refute what they (Kaczynski's mother and brother) said about you as well as provide a serious forum for your ideas."

"No one can dispute that you are an extremely smart man."

"I understand that you have moved to Colorado." (Well, involuntarily. Kaczynski is in prison in Colorado.)

It is important to treat everyone with respect. During the presidential campaign of 2000, a reporter asked George W. Bush to name the leaders of several nations. He could not and for several days the media feasted on Bush's ignorance. But many media critics and ordinary people thought the questioning tactic was smart-alecky. It reinforced a view among many that the media is arrogant.

A better line of questioning might have been to ask a short, open-ended question such as how Bush viewed recent developments in a specific country. Or, the reporter could have asked a specific question – how did the ascension to power of a certain leader fit into his foreign policy?

The answers to both of those questions would have revealed Bush's ignorance on foreign affairs without drawing scorn on the media.

Be interested, courteous, cool and confident. Never get into a debate with a subject. Even after a contentious interview, thank the person you have interviewed because he or she has given you a valuable gift – their time. It's up to us as journalists to make good use of that.

Be patient. In his book "Off Camera," Ted Koppel relates how it took him six years to persuade investor Warren Buffett to sit for an interview. You may not get the interview you want today, but you can begin to build a foundation of trust that will lead to an interview tomorrow.

Chapter 1.4

Sifting through the mountain

A reporter's life requires filtering though a clamor of voices wanting to be heard. Famed reporter and columnist Walter Lippmann probably did not envision the information stream that television and the internet would loosen, but what he said in 1920 about the role of a journalist endures: "The news of the day as it reaches the newspaper office is an incredible medley of fact, propaganda, rumor, suspicion, clues and hopes – and the task of selecting and ordering that news is one of the truly sacred and priestly offices in democracy."

Increasingly though, the bearers of these facts, propaganda, and other bits of information know how to reach us in sophisticated ways. Electronic services such as Business Wire and PR Newswire generate streams of news releases, all day, every day. More voices are heard by fax, e-mail, overnight delivery packages and regular mail. News services such as the Associated Press, Reuters, Bloomberg and Dow Jones churn out streams of news.

Others package their voice and their pictures in a video news release. These often are professionally done and can yield some B-roll we may want to use. But VNR's must be judged for what they are – a presentation with a self-serving message. Nothing wrong with that, as long as we realize it and use the information we get from these and other sources accordingly.

Sources

Every good reporter has an active and growing list of sources. Ideally, the station has an electronic source list that all reporters and producers can access and update. But that should not be a substitute for maintaining good contacts on our own. A good reporter is connected to the community he or she is covering in as many ways as possible. Good stories usually originate that way, not from news releases.

Many reporters content themselves with a contact file of "important people" – the mayor's chief of staff, a senior vice president at a big company in town, the coach of the university football team. Good reporters have a much deeper contact list than that. Their source file includes plenty of middle-level managers and also some ordinary folks who drive trucks, work a small farm or supervise a department in a store.

Why?

Because the upper echelon usually will give you only a tightly controlled company or party line. But the middle managers and the fellow working on the loading dock often have valuable information on how an organization really works.

Suppose you are doing a story on how a hospital is reorganizing. At a news conference to announce the changes, the hospital administrator and the chief of surgery explain the plan in glowing terms. You now have the official version. Not satisfied with that, you call a nursing supervisor you have cultivated. She tells you the reorganization will mean patients lacking health insurance no longer will be treated but rather will be sent elsewhere. Think about how much stronger your story now has become.

Background, not for attribution, and off the record

Often in reporting stories such as the one just mentioned, sources will insist on confidentiality. The nurse, for example, does not want to incur the wrath of the hospital administrator. In cases where wrongdoing or other legal issues may emerge, be sure you know your state's shield law and have consulted your station's lawyer before making such promises.

Know also the differences between "background," "not for attribution," and "off the record." Many reporters, producers, editors and anchors do not know the distinctions between those terms and even fewer sources will be able to detail the differences.

But a true journalistic professional must know.

"Background" means we may not use the source's name but may identify him or her organizationally using such terms as "a company source" or a "city official."

"Not for attribution" means the information cannot be linked even indirectly to the source because to do that might expose the source. We must find some other way to source or present the information. When you hear an anchor begin a news story with words such as "Action 4 News has learned..." you can be reasonably sure the station has obtained information "not for attribution" and failed to find a source to attribute that information.

"Off the record" means the information is for our understanding only. We may leverage that knowledge to obtain other information but we may not use the original information because to disclose it would compromise the source.

For example, only a candidate's physician and nurse might know certain information about the politician's medical history. Likewise, only the chief financial officer might know a company's internal fiscal dealings. In either case, if we as journalists were to violate an "off the record" agreement, one consequence might be that we have placed a doctor, nurse or company officer's job in jeopardy.

Remember, most people you will interview in the course of your reporting career will not know what "background," "not for attribution" and "off the record" means. They often will say "and this is off the record" and keep right on talking. We have not agreed to anything, so technically, everything is still on the record. To be fair though, we should ask them what they mean by that. Often, they just don't want their name associated with whatever they are telling you. They really mean background.

An elected official or officer of a publicly traded company will know the difference and will get your assent before being interviewed. But even in those cases, often a good reporter can convince the interviewee to go "on the record" for most of the interview. One way to do this is to go back after an "off the record" interview and specifically ask what the interviewee wants off the record and what can be on. Then probe further by asking why the interviewee wants certain parts off the record (even if it seems obvious to you). Often you will be able to assure them that whatever they wanted off the record won't harm them, and will ultimately improve the public's understanding of the story. You'll end up with much more "on the record" information that way, and a better story.

Keep this key guideline in mind when a source asks for something to be off the record: Your first answer should be no, and if they persist, ask them why.

Chapter 1.5

Live shots

Everything these days seems to be moving at a faster pace than ever before. Drivers run a credit card through a reader on the gasoline pump so they can get in and out of the station faster. Photo processing outlets develop and print our pictures in an hour. More and more stores stay open 24 hours a day so customers can get what they want now. No one wants to wait for anything.

And television news increasingly turns to the live shot both as a way to bring the viewers the very latest and just for the sake of being *live*! News directors are so enamored with live shots that the technique is deployed more and more to give viewers the illusion things are happening *now*!

Creating the live shot

The challenge for the reporter in a live shot is to sound and look smart, often with little information. Often, a reporter will screech to a stop at the scene of a fire, riot or other breaking news event and be expected to deliver a live shot as soon as the photographer fires up the camera and cranks up the antenna. With little time to report and none to write, the reporter must learn to compose on the fly, working from a few notes scribbled onto a note pad.

This requires superb thinking and writing skills. Rarely will a reporter have time to write something out. What the reporter must do is learn to write sentences in his or her head and then deliver them while making at most a few glances at hand-held notes.

Unfortunately, many reporters open their live shots by either repeating what the anchor has said in introducing them, or they tell the viewers what they can plainly see for themselves. These soliloquies often begin "As you can see behind me... ."

Even when severely pressed for time, good reporters strive to bring something new to their report, something not obvious to the viewer.

Let's say you roll up to the scene of a fire. With one sweep, the camera can tell viewers about the size of the building, how many fire trucks are working, and if injured people are being treated. Try to find out something that will make the live shot memorable. Is it a historic building? Have arson investigators been summoned? What is inside that might have ignited the blaze?

Press yourself to work quickly, drill yourself to simplify, learn to write "in your head" from your notes and you will be able to execute a good live report.

Tips for crafting a professional live shot

Stand slightly angled to the camera. This invites the viewer to look beyond you and will make your gestures and references to what's going on seem more natural. Facing the camera straight on looks confrontational.

Focus intently on what you are doing and saying. Enunciate your words precisely. Tune everything else out – noisy equipment, people at the scene yelling or waving.

Get right to the point – tell what's new first. This is counter to what most television reporters do – they set the scene first, often repeating what the anchor has said. But putting the news first makes the live shot more compelling and succinct.

Above all, explain. Tell the viewers why and how. Avoid lapsing into truisms. Make your live shot substantive and memorable by telling viewers something they don't already know or that isn't clearly obvious. Give some background; guide the viewers to what will happen next.

Refer to your notes by glancing down at them. Viewers expect to see a notebook. After all, you are a reporter. Outline very briefly your main points and the beginning, middle and end of what you are going to say. Avoid reading your notes; instead, make a very brief outline and use your thumb as a place mark.

If the anchor already has said it, we don't need to repeat it or to confirm it. ("That's right, Chris.")

Remember to pace yourself; don't race in an attempt to attach urgency to your report. Listen intently to people you are interviewing.

Make your movements purposeful. Many reporters have been told that movement, any movement, gives their stand-ups a dynamism missing from a stand-up in one place. So they employ what's called the "walk to nowhere," a stroll from point A to point B with no purpose other than to be moving. Think of your stand-up as your moment to explain, to demonstrate, to teach.

Practice, even if you only have a few minutes.

The clip-on mike is less intrusive and allows you to be more natural than the hand-held stick mike with the pie-plate station flags. And no need to shout – your mike will pick up your voice fine and will catch much less background noise than your ear can hear.

Conclude by saying your location, your name and your station in the format your station prescribes. "In Placerita Canyon, I'm Jimmy Joe Meeker, KTV News." Resist the temptation to add "now back to you

in the studio." Where else would we go? To a cartoon? Besides, the "back to you" phrasing abruptly shifts our communication with the viewers to a private conversation with our colleagues.

Hold your gaze steady on the camera. Keep that gaze for a few seconds after you think the live shot is finished. The anchor may come back with a question, and even if not, if you look away quickly, it distracts the viewers, who naturally want to know what stole your attention so quickly.

Refrain from scratching any part of your body.

Live shot conflicts

Going live means we must confront challenges of balance, fairness, and accuracy.

Going live does give the viewers an immediacy that is lost in a taped package. But going live also has many potential problems for the reporter. For one, we have far less control over what is broadcast than we do when we tape something. If someone we are interviewing live curses, for example, that's the way it goes out over the air. Other potential problems:

■ Claims made on live television cannot be verified.

■ Bystanders waving or shouting can distract the viewers.

■ Many politicians, business leaders and sports figures know how the media works and are very skilled at staging events.

How do we fairly represent the other side if they are not standing right next to us? It's up to us to provide that balance and fairness.

Developing a broadcast voice

Doing a live shot, reading a script on radio or delivering a newscast on television requires not just good reporting and writing but also a smooth, well-modulated voice. Otherwise, listeners and viewers will focus on our verbal idiosyncrasies and not the story.

In broadcasting today in the United States, regional accents practically have disappeared, replaced by consistent, middle-America pronunciations. The thinking is that regional variations in speech might cause some viewers to pay more attention to how the words are being said than to what it said.

At first, most reporters are nervous about speaking on camera and having their voice recorded.

Relax.

Only the most supremely egotistical listen to their first broadcast and say, "Hey, I'm really good!" The rest of us – the normal people – fret and stew that our voices sound terrible and we look even worse.

It's a two-step process to overcome that feeling. The first is to learn techniques that facilitate good delivery. The second is to become comfortable with your voice, your mannerisms, yourself.

Finding a broadcast voice that is you is harder than it may seem. Many beginning broadcasters stumble into a delivery pattern characterized by rhythmic rising and falling, punched-up words and rising inflection at the end of most sentences. It sounds artificial – and it is.

Other broadcast journalists adopt a near-theatrical delivery, which brings undue attention to them and detracts from the story, which is where we want our viewers and listeners to be focusing.

Remember that you are a storyteller. Tell your story in a natural cadence with emphasis where it would be if you were telling the story to a group around a campfire, or whatever setting you envision.

"We all know how to tell a good story to a friend," says broadcast voice coach Ann S. Utterback. "We might raise our pitch when we want to stress a word, and we might stretch some words out and say others faster. We do this naturally because of the feedback we get from our friend when we are talking. Creating a person to talk with helps these same qualities become part of broadcast delivery."

Tips to help develop your own broadcast voice

■ Speak at a comfortable pace but a little faster than perhaps you might normally. That will help give your delivery a little extra energy.

■ Relax and concentrate on precise enunciation.

■ Find your optimum tone by humming until you hear the best resonance.

■ Be genuinely interested in what you are talking about. Viewers and listeners will know immediately if you are merely going through the motions.

■ Make your movements deliberate and natural.

■ Correct your mistakes quickly and smoothly. That will be the most natural to your audience. Avoid scrunching your face, sighing, giggling or losing your composure in any way.

■ Pause between elements of your story or between stories. This will clearly signal your audience that you are changing topics.

Chapter 1.6

Producing the newscast

Putting together a newscast that is informative, compelling, engaging and interesting is one of journalism's great challenges. It's like preparing a great meal: all of the individual items must be good, and they should be presented in an appealing way. A flea on the salad can spoil the rest of the meal.

A newscast is a delicate mix of items, just like that good meal. Putting the segments together in an engaging manner is the producer's task.

Conventional wisdom in broadcasting says your lead story will determine how many listeners or viewers will stick with your station for the rest of the newscast. However, at all-news stations and on web sites, nothing really leads the newscast because listeners and viewers are coming and going all the time. Even so, the half-hour newscast remains the standard for local stations around the nation, and it's important to know how such a newscast is created.

First of all, we generally only have 22 minutes to work with – the rest of the half hour is given to commercials. Typically, the half-hour will contain four two-minute commercial breaks.

The producer must decide on the order and mix of the newscast – how to structure the packages, live shots, voice-overs, weather, sports and business in a way that is engaging and makes sense.

Like the top headline on a newspaper, the story chosen to lead the newscast says a lot about your station's news judgment and values. Given access to the same reporting, one station in your town might choose to lead with a story about an elderly woman attacked by dogs, a rival station might lead with a legislative development affecting school programs.

Let's say you are the news producer in charge of a certain newscast.

A good question to ask yourself is "what story is most broadly interesting and significant to our listeners or viewers?" Often, the quality of the pictures is a key factor in that decision. A strongly visual story often will bump a more thoughtful piece from the lead because the thinking is powerful pictures will capture the viewers and induce them to stay for the duration of the newscast.

Try to arrange your newscast so viewers are rewarded for sticking with you. Not every story can throb with energy or be drenched with emotion, but you can sprinkle little gems throughout the newscast. Tell your audience what you must but do it with as much grace and style as you can muster.

Connecting the segments

Beginning producers (and some who should know better) often fall to the temptation of trying to hitch together the stories in a newscast as if it were an episodic play. It's a good idea to group the items in the newscast in some sort of logical order, but avoid the trap of trying to connect unrelated stories with a thin string of false transitions.

A few years ago, a television sportscaster was dismissed for alluding that athletes resembled monkeys. The sportscaster's ill-advised remarks were an attempt to connect with the previous piece on chimpanzees at the local zoo.

Although you want to group related stories, there's no reason to try to stitch together what can't be linked. Imagine how foolish it would sound if in the course of a conversation between friends about the weather one said: "And speaking of rain, it looks like I'm getting soaked on my investment in General Products Industries."

Think of your radio or television audience as a group of your friends. A pause and change in inflection are enough to carry us to the next story.

Teases

Teases are an important part of broadcast journalism. Seminars are devoted to the writing of these references to what is coming in the newscast. They can be sprinkled into breaks in programming before the news, but most often they are used to lead into a commercial break. The purpose is to leave the audience so intrigued that they will not even flip through other channels during the commercial break for fear of missing a single second.

Oftentimes though, teases are so pumped up that they sound as if a huckster rather than a journalist wrote them.

"Will a new scientific breakthrough change life as we know it?

51

We'll tell you when we come back!"

"A local man is suspected of brutal crimes against orphans, widows and puppies – find out right after the break!"

"Is Hurricane Hattie going to devastate our city? Carol Cumulus is next with the weather!"

Telling the audience what will follow a break is a good service but leave the theatrics to carnival barkers. (Read more about teases in chapter 2.1).

Section 2
Writing

Chapter 2.1

Writing the script: The big picture

To some, writing for broadcast is more mechanical and confining than writing for print. Print reporters dabbling in broadcast sometimes chafe at what seem like limitations, such as the requirement that attribution be at the beginning of a sentence. But these requirements are there for good reason. If a newspaper reader misses the point of a sentence, he can go back and read it again. Someone listening to the radio or watching TV can't do that.

The radio news writer must ensure that the news copy is simple enough that the listener will understand immediately. The television news writer has the same responsibility, with the added complexity of dealing with pictures, bites, natural sound, and graphics needed to tell the story properly.

Broadcast news stories are short, especially when compared to newspaper and web stories. A newspaper can present hundreds of stories at once and a web site can offer access to a limitless number of stories. A television or radio station can only offer one story at a time. That restriction compels the broadcast journalist to be concise. Failure to keep the stories tight can drive away the audience. Anything we can excise or condense without diluting the meaning is generally a good practice.

A typical television news story runs about 90 seconds – about half a dozen paragraphs. These packages, as they are called, typically include an anchor introduction, video that the reporter voices over, and sound bites from some of the people interviewed for the piece.

This chapter deals with the first steps in broadcast writing – organizing a story and preparing to write. The subsequent chapters in Section 2 focus on the mechanics and tools of writing.

Preparation

The broadcast reporter must determine the dimensions of the story – how much reporting will be required – before heading out to the street. And the television field reporter typically also must figure out whether to include a stand-up and what it should cover.

After returning to the studio from the field, the reporter's first task is to log all the tape that has been shot (see the sample Video Tape Log reproduced on page 56). The reporter notes the time code for all the pieces of B-roll, nat (natural) sound, and bites. Time code, which is indicated in hours, minutes, seconds, and frames, is embedded on broadcast tape so that reporters and editors can find precisely where an edit should be.

B-roll, the pictures over which the reporter narrates, usually does not need to be noted as precisely on a script as the bites. However, you should note on your log sheet whether the pictures you have on tape are long shots, medium shots, or detail shots (close-ups).

Your log could look something like this:

Time code	Subject
00:41	Long shot – Children playing in park
01:03	Medium shot – Timmy on slide
01:20	Close-up of Timmy's foot in a cast
01:43	Bite: Timmy – I just wanted to play
01:47	End of bite... with the bigger kids
02:15	Nat sound of playground bell ringing`

And so on.

It also helps to note which shots go together, which will make it easier to assemble a story that unfolds smoothly. Make sure that you have a good mix of wide, medium and close-up, or detail shots.

With your log complete, you are now ready to sketch an outline of your story (see sidebar on outline writing). In doing this for television, consider your strongest pictures. As a general rule, lead with those, especially for a breaking news story.

Avoid leading with a stand-up – it's strong pictures that will attract and hold the viewers for the story. Viewers naturally expect pictures of what the anchor just suggested they were going to see. Save your smiling face for later in the piece when you want to explain a concept or connect ideas in your story.

Avoid also using B-roll of people talking. It's done all the time in TV news but it's contrary to what we naturally expect – that if we see people on screen with their lips moving we will be able to hear what they are saying.

Video Tape Log

TITLE		DATE
TAPE #	BUREAU #	EDITOR
TECHNICAL COMMENTS		CREW
TIME CODE ☐YES ☐NO	AUDIO CH 1	AUDIO CH 2

HOUR	MIN.	SEC.	SCENE

Graphic Request

Producer Jeff Rowe

Show/Segment 612

Air Date 22-23 JR

Edit Date _____

Description: 2 graphics for story on OC research project that has cut water use by 1/3 and resulted in stronger, taller trees

Christmas Tree production
in California

1. San Diego $4 million
2. San Mateo* $3.5 million
3. Riverside $2.8 million
4. Santa Clara $2.5 million
5. Orange $2 million

Christmas tree sales
1980 — 30 million
1990 — 36.2 million

Terms

Here are some of the basic terms and acronyms broadcast journalists need to know:

Bites – People speaking on tape. Called *actualities* or *sound cuts* in radio, *quotes* in print.

B-roll – All the pictures taken for the piece lacking featured sound; that is, a bite or natural sound you want to use in your story. These pictures are what the reporter uses to illustrate and voice over.

Closer – The concluding passage of a story, which should bring the story to a conclusion. It includes the reporter sign-off – "In Parkville, I'm Jon Hilera for KCSU News" – typically done over B-roll.

Package – A complete story with B-roll, VO, bites and reporter stand-up.

SOT – Sound on tape. Usually a synonym for bite. Nat sound refers to natural noise – dogs barking, a waterfall, engine racing, a crowd cheering.

Stand-up – The stand-up is the reporter-on-camera segment that typically is either:

■ A bridge, in which the reporter links elements of the story. Good writers clearly signal these transitions: "Some disagree," "Across town, the perception is different," or "But the agency says the mayor never attended the meeting" are examples.

■ An explainer, where the reporter presents information on concepts, issues or emotions that are difficult to depict with even the best pictures.

■ A closer, in which the reporter concludes or sums up the story and adds his or her name. "In Carney, I'm Loralei Rodriguez."

Sometimes, a determining factor in deciding what our stand-up will be is a lack of B-roll – pictures to cover a certain part of the story.

VO – Voice Over. The voice track recorded over the pictures (B-roll).

Remember that our script should explain the pictures rather than describe them. Our script should add to what viewers are watching to help them understand. At a fire, for example, the pictures will show viewers clearly how high the flames are. We want to enhance the viewers' experience by supplying facts not visible. "The fire was so big, a jetliner landing 70 miles away spotted it from the air." Or, "The water was so deep, cars disappeared from view."

It's good to refer directly to the pictures when appropriate. ("This odd-looking helicopter is called a Sikorsky Skycrane.")

And we can add perspective to the pictures. In a winter river rescue story, we could point out the average survival time given the temperature of the water.

Sometimes, it's best to be quiet. The late David Brinkley was respected for his writing – and also for his discipline in remaining silent when the pictures told the story. He tried to add insight and background to the pictures; otherwise, he was silent.

Often, the only pictures available are routine. A defendant walking into court. People sitting in a meeting. Someone being handed an award. We have to work even harder in those cases to find something interesting about the event. ("For the first time since the trial began, Dennis McKenna wore a suit." "The people at this meeting waited up to four hours to speak." "Pablo Fila had never won anything in his life until today.")

Look upon "routine" stories as special challenges. Somehow, we must find something interesting, something that teaches people something new, that makes their time spent watching our newscast worthwhile.

Years ago, when Prince Charles and Princess Diana still were together, news footage from the networks arrived showing the royal couple posing with their skis, getting on a lift, poling toward the lodge. Boring, cliché

Bites and SOTs

In television news, the quote on tape is called "sound bite" or simply a "bite." It's also called a SOT, for "sound on tape." Whatever you call it, the best ones are those in which our interview subject speaks from a strong emotion, closely held ideal, entrenched belief, or just-discovered revelation.

And the best bites usually are short ones; paraphrase the long explanations in your own narrative track and keep the bites in your news package tight and strong. "That's baloney! I wasn't there!" is a strong bite; a detailed explanation of the speaker's whereabouts probably is not.

As a general guideline, look for ways to cut the bite once it gets to ten seconds. Longer than that, and it had better be a very compelling bite. "Aim for objective copy and subjective sound," advises Al Tompkins, group leader for broadcast and online at the Poynter Institute, a school for journalists in St. Petersburg, Fla. So the reporter voice over might read: "Witnesses say the men jumped out of the car, chased down the victim and emptied their guns into him as he pleaded for his life." Followed by a witness bite: "It was like watching a pack of wolves. The men who shot him are barbaric savages."

Jump cuts – Two bites from the same person spliced together typically will require a bit of B-roll to cover the last few words of the first bite and the first few of the second bite. Otherwise, the image "jumps" between bites on the screen and becomes what is called a "jump cut." These also can be avoided by "dissolves," "wipes," "tumbles," and other editing and graphic techniques that can smooth the transition and signal to the viewer that the bites were taken from different parts of the interview.

When we use B-roll to cover a jump cut, we must take great care to make sure we have not distorted the speaker's meaning by putting together bites spoken at different times during the interview or on-scene taping.

Introducing the speaker – Most television news programs use on-screen name and title lines to identify speakers. (*60 Minutes* is an exception.) These names and titles are called fonts, a reference to type styles, or CGs, for character generator, the computer that creates them on screen.

This on-screen identification means we do not have to formally introduce the speakers in our script. A transition sentence may be required however – "Some tenants remain angry at the owner."

shots – until the end of the feed, which showed a group of reporters stumbling, tripping and falling in the snow as they tried to keep up with the royal couple. Think how much more memorable, revealing and funny it would be for the viewers if the piece focused on the reporters struggling to cover the royals.

On the script, note also what graphics are wanted (see the sample Graphic Request form reprinted on page 57). Depending on the size of your station and the depth of the staff, you may be able to get some exotic and sophisticated graphics. At smaller stations, you may be limited to type on screen. Use graphics judiciously – although they can be valuable in helping viewers understand, too many of them can exasperate a viewer.

Now you are almost ready to write your piece, but pause once more: Ask yourself what tone your story should take, and what the main theme will be. How will you approach the topic? How should you handle the elements of your story? Consider how you can build a little surprise into the story. Perhaps it is a bit of natural sound, an unexpected turn in the story, or something that brings a different level of drama to the report.

We have several different story formats to choose from:

■ **Inverted pyramid**: Good for breaking news and "just-the-facts-ma'am" stories. Begins with a summary lead and proceeds with details in descending order of importance.

■ **Narrative**: Step-by-step storytelling. Novels typically are written this way. Good for stories where one step leads to the next, such as how police solved a crime.

■ **Gold coins along the trail**: Reveal the story a significant element at a time, not necessarily in time order the way a narrative does. The listener, viewer or reader is rewarded for staying with the story by learning ever more compelling elements (the gold coins) as the reporter leads the viewers along the story trail, the way a mystery movie might do. Good for stories with multiple strong elements, such as the factors contributing to homelessness in a city or how an uneducated immigrant woman in a poor, tough neighborhood mobilized her neighbors to fight gangs.

Narratives and the "gold coins" story forms make good use of foreshadowing and other literary devices not typically found in straight-ahead inverted pyramid reporting. For more on these literary devices, see chapter 2.3.

Make sure you have pictures for everything you write and that your timing works out correctly. Most newsroom computer systems have a feature that ticks off as you write how long it will take to read what you have written. These typically are calibrated for a fast reader, so you may have to allow more time for what you have written than the computer indicates. For example, to end up with 60 seconds of on-screen material, you may find that you have to stop at what the computer says is 50 seconds.

Story lead

Many reporters devote great effort to crafting a good "lead," or opening to their story. It not only sets the tone for the piece but also determines whether the listener or viewer sticks with us. Your journalistic "tool box" contains several types of leads:

■ **Summary or theme:** These state the story premise directly. "People who live near the city dump are getting the flu at twice the rate of people elsewhere in the city and doctors blame infectious wastes." Or, "In a land of pain, the children suffer the most." Or, "Martians landed earlier today at Tomorrowland."

The summary or theme leads often are the simplest, yet they typically are the most effective because they make an immediate emotional connection with the listeners and viewers.

■ **Hard news:** A variation of the summary/theme lead. The hard news lead states the latest news in straight-ahead fashion. "Two people nearly drowned today when a wave capsized their sailboat off Treasure Island."

■ **Anecdotal or scene-setter:** These deliver a scene or character from the story in the expectation it will lure the viewer, listener, or reader into sticking with the story to find out what happens.

> "Five-year old Chris Dupalier walked to the park next to his house Tuesday morning, just as he had many times before to play with his friends. It was a warm, sunny day, with no hint of danger."

Or,

> "Tears cascaded down Gloria Sagon's cheeks and splashed onto the cracked glass of the frame bearing the picture of her brother, Anthony."

An anecdotal lead counts on attracting the viewer or listener to that element of the story we highlight at the beginning. It's over-used and thus many anecdotal leads sound off-the-shelf. For an anecdotal lead to work, it must be relevant to the theme, simple, focused and foreshadow what is to come.

Here's a spoof, but it's close to what many reporters write:

Writing the script: The big picture

Gregg Jackson pushed back the remains of the platter of linguini and considered the question as he wiped the dripping tomato sauce from his rubbery lips, first with the left sleeve, then with the right.

But before he could speak, a powerful burp, welling up from the depths of his distended abdomen, vibrated his flaccid cheeks and hissed through his flared nostrils.

It had been that kind of night for the American League's second-place team, the Boomers.

"We just got beat," the Boomer skipper said.

And so they did...

In real life, such leads might be better reserved for an evening of storytelling around the campfire.

In some instances though, an anecdotal lead can work very well. A story in *The Wall Street Journal* about people on second marriages taking their combined children along on their honeymoon began this way:

Nicholas Spaccarotelli had a blast on his recent honeymoon on the Oregon coast. He took long walks on the beach, enjoyed breathtaking ocean views from his cozy cabin, and lingered over dinners in front of the fireplace.

Nicholas is 12. He and his brother, Mario, 10, came along on the honeymoon after their father, Chris, remarried. "It was so cool," said Nicholas.

Coming soon to a heart-shaped bathtub near you: The familymoon.

That lead worked very well because it foreshadowed, hinted at the theme, and contained a surprise. Engaging as that is for print, the broadcast writer lacks the luxury of time it would take to read all that. The broadcast writers lead must be compressed into a sentence for the anchor that is both factual and creates a bit of mystery that will induce the listener or viewer to stick around. So the anchor lead might be:

Changing demographics is altering how newlyweds honeymoon. Our reporter looks into the familymoon.

The reporter then might open the piece with a sentence on how Nicolas and his younger brother enjoyed their recent honeymoon trip.

■ **Question lead:** These strive to engage our audience by mentally getting them to answer "yes" to the question we ask. Use these sparingly for two reasons: too many question leads can make the newscast sound like a quiz; and, listeners, viewers and readers will abandon the story if their mental answer to the question lead is "no."

A story that opens "Do you worry about having enough money for retirement?" will engage those who are worried but it will leave everyone else searching for the channel changer.

In all leads, restrain the hyperbole.

And if we cannot stop ourselves from using "massive," "giant" or some other inflated and vague term, make sure the next sentence specifies the actual size of whatever we have described as "massive."

We should avoid labeling the news in any way: Surprising, disturbing, amazing, shocking, good news or bad. Let the listeners and viewers draw their own conclusions.

The heart of the story

When writing the main part of your story, keep in mind a few basic guidelines:

■ Bites typically follow and amplify a point made in your script. For example, a story on bee attacks might proceed this way:

Script (your voice): "Experts advise covering your eyes, nose and mouth."

Bite: "Those are the sensitive areas that the bees seek out."

■ Avoid what are called "echo quotes." These essentially repeat what was just said.

So for example, if your script says "The crew then heard the metal scraping," you want to avoid a bite following it that says "Then we heard metal screeching."

Better to find a bite that amplifies your script such as "It sounded like two boats in pain."

■ Use silence in television reporting. Few reporters do this, thinking they must talk over every second of tape.

But sometimes a silent pause after a particularly emotional bite enables the viewers to absorb what was said. And the moments of natural sound – the wind blowing across the high plains or the rain beating on a roof can set the tone of a story far better than our words.

In discussing plans for President Reagan's funeral in June 2004, the anchors of the major American television news networks all agreed on the importance of silence. In an interview with the *Philadelphia Inquirer*, Peter

Writing the script: The big picture

Jennings of ABC said his father taught him that on such occasions "you must let people hear the horses' hooves." During the funeral procession, Jennings let the viewers hear and absorb much more than the horses hooves. Beyond identifying people, he said little. Neither did Dan Rather at CBS or Tom Brokaw at NBC, who said the pictures "speak for themselves on these occasions."

■ Digress, but only briefly. Listeners and viewers will stick with you for a brief side trip during your story but if you stay too long, they will get confused. So for example, in a story on a soccer player's quest for the goals scored record, it is certainly pertinent to note that the player lived for a time as boy in a foster home. But if we stay on that topic for more than a sentence or two, our audience will get lost. Mentally they will ask themselves, "Is this story on the record chase or the player's childhood?"

■ Write in a positive way rather than a negative one – not to be boosterish but because it's often more precise to say what something is rather that what it is not.

For example, "neither studio would say whether they would proceed" conveys more information than "neither studio would comment."

Especially avoid double negatives such as "not uncommon." Those force the listener, viewer and reader to stop and think about what is really meant. So let's replace, "It was no surprise when the train rumbled though town" with, "Right on time, the train rumbled through town." We've made our sentence more precise and lopped off two words. Less can be more in broadcast news writing.

After you have finished writing, read your script aloud quietly. Hearing it is the best way to identify words, phrases or sentences that just don't work right. Reading aloud also is a great way to identify words or phrases that you have trouble pronouncing. Better to discover them when you have a chance to rewrite than when you are on the air.

The goal is a finished piece that flows as smoothly as a song.

Your next task is to "track" your script; that is, read what you have written while an editor tapes it. In recording all voice tracks, remember to count down "3 - 2 - 1" before you begin speaking. This allows the tape editor to start the track precisely.

When you are finished writing, tracking and getting your graphics, the editor's work begins. At small stations, that also could be you.

The editor's job is to take your script and lift all the B-roll, bites, graphics and other elements you have indicated and arrange them on a fresh tape in the order you have prescribed.

When the editor is finished, a television news package is born, awaiting only the anchor lead and tag.

Outlining

When I was about six years old, I got a wristwatch for Christmas. It came with a small, folded piece of paper telling me how to wind the watch (not too tightly) and how to change the time (pull out the stem and turn it.) That was it.

A few years ago, I received another watch as a gift. The instruction book ran 72 pages.

In almost every way, life has become more complex. It's our job as journalists to sort out the complexities for our viewers, listeners and readers. This means we often have to sift through a great deal of often-convoluted material and distill it into something that makes sense. Look upon this part of reporting as a process of putting the pieces of a puzzle together.

In doing this, you will find it will help enormously to make a brief outline before you begin writing. For long or multi-part stories, an outline is a must, but even on short stories, the few minutes you spend putting together a brief outline will greatly speed the writing process.

Your outline should include:

■ The lead element – how you will intrigue the listener and viewer.

■ The theme, or nut graph – what the story is about, why the listener and viewer should care.

■ Supporting facts, reasons and logic – the evidence that reinforces the theme.

■ History – what happened that led to the current story.

■ Scope – how widespread the development is.

■ Impact – who or what is affected.

■ Opposition, conflict – who or what is acting to counter the forces in the story.

■ Future – what could happen next?

Anchor lead

An anchor lead is a sentence or two that sets up the story and introduces the reporter. Here's an example:

A sheriff's helicopter rescued two men earlier today from Mount Santiago. Jim Braver explains how the men survived the crash of their homebuilt aircraft.

Such a straightforward approach works well with breaking news and much of the reporting of day-to-day events. But for an enterprise piece, we want to strive to include a bit of mystery, a hint as to what the story will reveal. Here's an example:

> Some graduate students at the University of California Irvine got a lesson today in the criminal justice system – they were arrested and hauled off to jail, just as they had planned. Our reporter explains.

That lead tells the listener or viewer a bit about the story and provides an incentive for them to keep listening or watching – the mystery will be revealed.

Anchor tag

The anchor tag is the concluding bit of information the anchor reads after the reporter has closed out the package or signed off from the field. Typically, these tie up any loose ends or tell us what will happen next. ("The trial is scheduled to begin next week.")

A tag also may give a bit of information or perspective that helps cement the story in the viewer's mind. ("If he had survived, little Joey would have celebrated his fifth birthday next Tuesday.") The tag also may refer the viewer to where more information can be found – for example, a web site or a telephone number.

Avoid tags that communicate the obvious ("We will have more on this story as it develops"). Also, find something better than a platitude ("Parents are urged not to keep matches where children can reach them"); or an on-air credit ("Thanks for that report, Eduardo"). Give the listener and viewer real information.

Not every story needs an anchor tag. But we should write one anyway, just in case the producer needs a few more seconds in the segment. Professionals always do the little extra things that help make the newscast strong and memorable.

Teases

Perhaps no element of broadcast news is more lampooned than teases, those references to stories ahead in the newscast. Writing teases has become a growth industry, with more varieties springing up all the time. We have the next-story tease, the mystery tease, the question tease, natural sound or sound bite teases, exclusives and warning teases.

Some evidence suggests viewers hate teasers. A study by John Carey at Greystone Communications suggests that rather than retain viewers and listeners, teasers actually repel them. But it will take more than a study or two to wean news directors from teasers, especially when even a small nudge in the ratings can mean thousands of dollars in ad revenue – and the news director's job.

But we certainly can do a better job with teases.

We can make sure a tease tells what the upcoming story is about and why viewers should care. We can promise to tell the how and why. We can avoid hyperbole – the "biggest," the "fastest," the "first of its kind" – because such words and phrases have lost meaning from overuse. We can avoid those so overtly hyped a flim-flam man would blush:

"Will the hurricane come ashore in our town and destroy life as we know it?! We'll tell you right after the break!"

That's hucksterism, not journalism.

SUPER TREE   House Number:

Video	Audio
Anchor intro:	THAT CHRISTMAS TREE IN YOUR LIVING ROOM IS ONE OF ABOUT 36 MILLION SOLD THIS YEAR -- RAISING AND SELLING THE TREES IS BIG BUSINESS AND AN ORANGE COUNTY RESEARCHER HAS FIGURED OUT A WAY TO GROW CHRISTMAS TREES FASTER, STRONGER AND BUSHIER. ORANGE COUNTY REGISTER REPORTER JEFF ROWE HAS MORE.
B-roll - tape 2 In: 00:38 sign; and 11:16 greenhouse	This is the university of california farm research station in irvine, where among dozens of projects, janet hartin has found out how to grow christmas trees faster and using far less water.
In: 28:48 These trees have . . . Out: 28:55 . . . tree farm	Bite: Janet Hartin, UC Researcher
Graphic on tree sales	Christmas tree sales have risen steadily in the US, climbing from 30 million in 1980 to 36 million last year.
Graphic on tree production	And orange county ranks fifth in california in christmas tree production. But it's dry here and water is expensive.
In: In 29:18 Because seasonally Out: 29:32 . . . than guessing	Bite: Janet Hartin
B-roll tape 1 -- In 26:55 gauge	Using these soil moisture gauges, hartin calculated exactly how much water each tree needs and when it needs it.
then, tape 2 - In: 02:20 overview of trees	that allows the tree to grow faster and fuller than if it got too little or too much to drink. water is expensive and for growers, water saved is money earned

SUPER TREE

House Number:

Video	Audio
In: 29:44 Once we convinced .. Out 29:54 . . . proof here	Bite: Janet Hartin
B-roll from michelle miller pack on christmas tree safety - box 2020	Profits have been flat for Christmas tree retailers in recent years but thanks to hartin's research, better years loom. for the orange county newschannel, i'm jeff rowe.
anchor tag:	NORMALLY, IT TAKES FOUR YEARS TO GROW A MONTEREY PINE CHRISTMAS TREE TO MARKET SIZE BUT HARTIN GREW THEM BIG ENOUGH IN JUST THREE YEARS

Chapter 2.2

Writing the script: The basics

Broadcast news writing differs from traditional newspaper writing in many ways, but if we had to distill the art and science of broadcast news writing into one sentence, it would be: Use simple, declarative sentences in this order – subject, verb, object.

The listener and viewer cannot go back and re-read a sentence like this one, which contains a clause, if they did not quite follow it when they heard it. So, broadcast writing must be the clearest of all communications:

■ It should be concise.

■ It should be told through the strongest characters our reporting can deliver.

■ It should distill a pile of details into simple descriptions.

■ It should explain the complex in easy-to-understand steps.

■ It should focus on a story that leads to a clear summation, or conclusion.

■ It should be constructed with a beginning, middle, and an end, which reveals a basic truth.

Getting to those basic truths requires great skill because only someone who thoroughly understands something can explain it simply. Leave the complex allegories to analytical pieces in print – the job of the broadcast journalist is to make an ever more complex world a little more understandable.

And we have relatively few words to communicate all this wisdom. Former network news writer Mervin Block, who now spends much of his time coaching, noted in one of his recent newsletters that an average edition of *The New York Times* contains about 250,000 words, about a thousand times as many words as a typical evening newscast.

So in broadcast we must do more with less. And the listener and viewer have no opportunity to re-read the script if it was not clear to them as they listened or watched.

Successful broadcast news writing requires mastering some different techniques that consider how people absorb information they hear and pictures they see.

Declarative sentences

An obituary in a major daily newspaper a few years ago began this way:

> Milton E. Mohr, former chairman, president and chief executive officer of the Los Angeles-based financial data firm Quotron Systems Inc., who was credited with moving the company from near bankruptcy to dominance of its market, has died at the age of 85.

Forget for a moment that we don't talk like that. Years ago, my sister called to tell me some news. She said: "Grandma died last night." Imagine my astonishment if my sister had said: "Grandma, who was never a pound overweight in her life and always remembered her Irish roots, died yesterday of heart failure. She was 94."

Granted, I knew my grandmother. But we simply don't communicate in real life with long suspended clauses like the one written for the Mohr obituary. What we might say, and what works well for broadcast news, is to write it this way:

> The man who built Quotron Systems into a leading financial data company died earlier this week. Milton Mohr was 85; he had been suffering from cancer. He died at his Malibu home.

Mid-sentence clauses force the listener and viewer to reassemble the sentence in their heads, a tough task when the anchors and reporters keep right on talking. At least in print, the reader can go back over sentences like the Mohr lead if they didn't grasp it on the first pass. Moreover, by introducing what Mohr had done before we introduced him by name made it easier for the listener to process.

Be kind to your listener's and viewer's brains. Give them the news one declarative sentence after another, all of them free of mid-sentence clauses.

Use real verbs...and keep them together

Choosing strong, appropriate verbs is the broadcast news writer's most powerful tool.

Omit verbs that are the literary equivalent of a flat tire. "Continue," "located" and "held" (as in meetings) almost always can be jettisoned. Consider how much stronger "parishioners will gather for the funeral tomorrow" is than "the funeral will be held tomorrow." Every use of "there is," "there was" and all other variations of the verb "to be" represents an opportunity squandered to use a strong, vivid verb.

Consider this sentence:

"The man has a large tattoo of a tiger on his right shoulder."

Nothing structurally wrong with that sentence, but think about how much more vivid it would be to write:

"A tattoo of a tiger straddles his right shoulder."

Network newscasts often begin with some variation of "there are new developments tonight... ." For now, forget the useless "tonight"; we'll deal with that shortly. Consider how much stronger, and more natural, it would be if we wrote instead what those developments are. "Palestinian leaders say they will come to Jerusalem... ."

An exception to our strong verb preference is "say." It's perfect for attribution. "Insisted," "warned," "disclosed," "promised" and dozens of other verbs are indeed stronger than "said." But they all carry a connotation, however slight, that makes "say" and "said" the most neutral choice for attribution. Reserve "according to" for documents. No human ever "accorded." And refrain from using "feel" as a synonym for "say." We only know what someone says, the words that actually tumble from their lips. Often what people say is very different from what they truly feel.

Consider Michael Eisner's appearance on CNN's Larry King show in

73

1996. The Walt Disney Company chief executive had been complaining to Disney executives and others that Michael Ovitz was a disaster as his second-in-command. As a way to get rid of Ovitz and avoid a payout, Eisner endeavored to persuade Sony Corp. to hire Ovitz to run its entertainment division. Then, to put a good face on that deal, Eisner went on the King show and said media reports of a rift between him and Ovitz were "baloney" and that given the chance, he would hire Ovitz again.

The ploy didn't work and a few months later, negotiations began on a severance package for Ovitz. In an email to Disney's public relations chief, Eisner described Ovitz as "totally incompetent," "untrustworthy" and a "psychopath." What he had *said* on the King show obviously wasn't what he *felt*.

Verbless sentences

Viewers of some newscasts in recent times could be forgiven if they concluded that verbs had gone way up in price. Some reporters and anchors are avoiding them, or substituting "-ing" gerunds and participles for real verbs. The goal is to produce more active-sounding sentences.

And so you hear "Movement tonight on the strike," or "A student in big trouble with his teacher," and "Snow in the mountains."

I serious. No verbs. They gone.

Verbless sentences might occasionally be useful in short teases, but beyond that, they comes off as an affectation. Here's an example broadcast news coach Deborah Potter used in an essay in the *Communicator*, a magazine for news directors:

"Cops and demonstrators clashing openly in the streets of the nation's capital, pepper spray, smoke bombs, night sticks beating back the crowds."

Potter writes: "That's not active copy. It's a run-on sentence fragment." As a wise person once said, the goal of good writing is to "express," not to "impress."

Finally, anything we can do to make it easier for the listeners and viewers to understand is something we want to do. Keep verb parts together in sentences. Rather than saying "... was also injured," say "... also was injured." It's smoother and easier to understand.

Tense

Broadcast journalism is mostly about what is happening now. Broadcast is the immediate medium; print the reflective one. So for example, the evening newscast might have a story about a late-afternoon school fire. The pictures would show firefighters aiming water at the flames; the copy would tell the viewers what burned, who was injured, and perhaps

Round off numbers

Make it easy on the listener.

Say "almost ten million dollars" instead of $9.86 million. The listener and viewer will be grateful and their understanding will increase because you have made the figures easier to register in the brain.

Remember though, that some numbers cannot be rounded off – the stock market close, for example. On television, though, we can help the viewer by putting those numbers on a graphic.

Avoid the phrases "less/fewer than" and "more than." Publicists often write "more than $50,000 was raised for the fight against (whatever)." Was it $50,001 or $50 billion? Simplifying numbers does not mean leaving listeners and viewers with an open-ended guess. Press the source to be specific – 99 percent of the time, you will be able to write "about 50 thousand dollars was raised." The same reasoning applies to "less than" or "fewer than." How much less? How many fewer?

Strive to reduce numbers in a broadcast story to the minimum. Anytime we can say "almost triple," "about half," or some similar comparison, we have made it easier for listeners and viewers to understand the story.

what fire inspectors theorized about the cause.

The print story the next morning (and the broadcast pieces) would have all that information, but ideally would focus more on the cause, condition of any injured, and where the students would attend class.

For broadcast news, we always want to be asking ourselves "what is the latest?" That said, we should try hard to avoid the epidemic in broadcast journalism of artificial present tense.

Consider these story leads:

"A disagreement turns deadly when..."

"Two men are dead after..."

"Fire guts a suspected crack house just after..."

Often these leads begin stories that are many hours old. But because news consultants have told station managers that present-tense story leads give listeners and viewers a sense of urgency, broadcast news writers simply have forced present tense.

Such a practice is unnatural, at least mildly deceptive, and not the way we communicate with other real humans. If a friend asks about the accident on the freeway, we wouldn't respond: "Two people are dead and six more are seriously injured in the crash of a rendering plant truck and busload of

Be careful – words can hurt

Some years ago, a young reporter at a small newspaper described a woman in a news story as "rather plain looking." A few days later, he received a letter from the "plain-looking" woman's husband. He told the reporter what a wonderful wife, mother and community volunteer the "plain-looking" woman was and how much he loved her.

The reporter said from that day forward he read his copy with this in mind: "If I was writing about my father, sister or other loved one, would my descriptions be fair?"

Broadcast writers don't have to sanitize their copy, but it's worth keeping the "plain-looking" woman in mind when we write.

orphans and widows." Rather, we would say something like "Two people were killed and six seriously hurt when... ."

If we absolutely are commanded to use present tense, then let's find out what is "present." What's new? In the freeway crash, it might be "Six people are expected to recover from injuries suffered when... ." For a later broadcast, our lead might be "two victims of that big freeway crash last night have gone home from the hospital but four others remain." Or, "A funeral mass is planned for Friday for one of the victims of yesterday's freeway crash that involved a truck and a bus. No word yet on services for the other victim killed when the truck tipped over as it... ."

In attempts to be current, strive mightily to avoid grotesque contortions such as "... is dead tonight." You would never tell a brother or sister that "grandma is dead tonight."

"Tonight" and "today" are sprinkled into broadcast news copy in the false belief that viewers will flee unless we keep reminding them that everything in the newscast is breathlessly new. And beware that meaning can change depending on where the "today" or "tonight" is inserted into the sentence. "Las Vegas is recovering from a flood tonight" means to most listeners that the flood was tonight. "Las Vegas is recovering tonight from a flood" means the flood was sometime before tonight.

Future and conditional tenses also often get mangled in broadcast news writing. "Will" expresses intent, a sense of certainly – as best as we can know it – that something is going to happen: "Congress will consider the bill when it returns from recess."

"Would" is conditional and needs at least an implied "if": "Congress would consider the bill if it is re-introduced."

Perfect tenses – or are they?

Another trouble zone in broadcast news writing are the perfect tenses – present perfect ("have" or "has" plus the verb), past perfect ("had" plus the verb) and future perfect ("will have" plus the verb).

Using the perfect tenses, we end up with sentences such as:

"Senator Krazeski has said she favors the legislation."

If you can do it without changing the meaning, replace the perfect construction "has said" with the simpler "says." It's easier for the listeners to digest and also brings joy to news directors pressured to make everything present tense.

So our new sentence reads: "Senator Krazeski says she favors the legislation."

Active vs. passive voice

Use active voice whenever possible. Active-voice sentence construction means the subject of the sentence is the originator of the action. Example: "Luis threw the ball."

Passive voice construction is the opposite – the subject of the sentence is receiver of the action. Example: "The ball was thrown by Carlene."

Besides being easier for the listener to follow, active voice sentences are livelier.

We can use passive voice when we want to emphasize the receiver of the action. Example: "Alderman Joe Smith was arrested for drunk driving tonight." The active sentence would be: "Police arrested Alderman Joe Smith for drunk driving tonight." That's not a bad sentence, but the emphasis shifts to the *police* who arrested Smith; what's news is that Smith was arrested.

Many writers lapse into passive voice, well, passively. On any given day, we can hear anchors saying sentences such as "concerns are being raised tonight..." or "the robber is described as... ." Better to say "parents are raising concerns…" and "police describe the robber as... ."

Unless we specifically want to put the emphasis on the receiver of the action, we will communicate much more clearly, vigorously and memorably using active voice.

Characters and titles

In broadcast news writing, make every word prove its worth. Broadcast news writing is a great example of "less is more." Dump every unnecessary word, phrase and sentence.

For example, print stories routinely use full names and titles to attribute information. But the more information we cram into a broadcast news

77

story, the greater the chance that the important information will be forgotten. So while a print story might refer to "Nancy Adams, a salinity expert with the National Oceanic & Atmospheric Administration," that's way too much detail for broadcast, where we want to focus only on what is central for our story to be understood. Is Adams a character our listeners and viewers need to know? Or do we have a bite we want to use from her? If not, let's drop her name and long title from our story and simply refer to her as a "government expert." If we do need her name, let's simplify her title to "oceans expert."

Similarly, we often can simplify long formal agency titles. A print story might say "U.S. Immigration and Customs Enforcement," but for broadcast we can shorten that to "the U.S."

If you do need to include a title, always put it before the name. So it's "United Carboration Chief Executive Frank McTeague said today he wants to..." and not, "Frank McTeague, chief executive of United Carboration, said today... ."

Paraphrasing

In print, writers have a number of sources of quotes – in-person interviews, phone interviews, and printed materials.

The broadcast journalist has just one source – what people have said into the microphone. For everything else, and even for much of what our sources say on tape, the broadcaster must paraphrase, distilling sometimes long, meandering comments into a terse sentence. That's all right, because our audience is better served when we condense big bags of information into a neat stack. We want the bites we use to be the emotional punctuation in our story, the points where people speak from the heart. For everything else, we can paraphrase.

If, for whatever reason, we fail to get that great sound bite, it's almost always better in broadcast writing to paraphrase. It's awkward to say: "The president said he knew, quote, 'nothing at all,' unquote, about how his intern would testify." An exception to this rule is if paraphrasing will dilute or obscure the meaning of what someone said. In those cases, it's better to attribute the specific remarks as "in her words."

If for example, the governor called the mayor of your town a "moron" in a public forum of some sort, it would be silly to recast that into "the governor questioned the mayor's intelligence." Better to write: "the governor used the word 'moron' in referring to the mayor."

Spell out everything

Newscasters reading your copy will be grateful. For example, spelling out everything will lessen the chance "St." will be pronounced as "saint" when the writer means "street." Writing "two million dollars" instead of "$2 million" reduces the chances an anchor will say "two dollars" if the copy line breaks between $2 and million.

Put attribution at the beginning of the sentence. It's OK in print to say: "The one-armed man could not be found anywhere in the vicinity of Kimble's house, police said." For the listener though, that's hard to follow. So, put the attribution at the beginning: "Police said the one-armed man could not be found anywhere in the vicinity of Kimble's house."

Generally, we want to attribute information in our reports. Viewers and listeners expect to be told the source of the facts we are presenting so they can evaluate its credibility. But when we have confirmation from several sources, we often can drop the attribution – at least in the lead.

And we can run generally accepted facts without attribution. It would sound silly if the weathercaster said "astronomers say dawn will come tomorrow at 6:15."

Pronouncers

A newscaster mispronouncing a word can damage the best broadcast story. And with more and more exotic locations and unfamiliar names popping into the news, providing pronunciation assistance is vital.

A pronouncer is simply a phonetic spelling of a name, place, or object or process that might be unfamiliar to the anchor. So, for example, rather than let the newsreaders stumble over the pronunciation of a multi-syllable name of someone from Eastern Europe, let's give them a pronouncer, which we usually in parenthesis.

And we need not confine pronouncers to long names from far away places. We should, for example note whether someone named "Colin" pronounces it "kah-lin" or "koe-lin."

Here's how to create a pronouncer:

For consonants, use:

K for the hard C as in cat

S for the soft C as in cease

SH for the soft CH as in machine

CH for the hard CH as in catch

Z for the hard S as in disease

S for the soft S as in sun

G for the hard G as in gang

J for the soft G as in general

For vowels, use:

AY for the long A as in gate

A for the short A as in far

AH for the short A as in father

AW for the broad A as in walk

EE for the long E as in greet

EH for the short E as in get

EYE for the long I as in time

EE for I when it sounds like a long E as in machine

IH for a short I as in city

OH for a long O as in vote

AH for a short O as in hot

AW for a broad O as in bought

EW or OO for a long U as in rule

UH for a short U as in shut

Here's an example of how pronouncers might be inserted into copy:

Chris Fernandez said he would meet with Che Matifataya (mah-tih-fuh-tay-uh) in Natchitoches (nah-kuh-dish), Louisiana and then would visit Bossier (boh-zur) city and Plaquemine (plah-kuh-min).

Using pronouncers is especially important for new anchors, who may be unfamiliar with the correct pronunciations of all the local people, places and customs.

Pronouncers would have been welcomed by a new anchor some years ago who read a story on air about Mater Dei high school, which she pronounced "may-ter die." The pronouncer would have helped the anchor say the name correctly – "mah-ter day" ("Mother of God" in Latin).

Chapter 2.3

Writing the script: The tools

Making the news interesting is where the craft of journalism comes into play. We learn to cull through our reporting to find the strongest facts to support our thesis and then we assemble them in a way that flows as smoothly as the Mississippi River on a summer day.

We're striving to avoid what CNN International Networks president Chris Cramer says is the "worst crime in journalism: the failure to make interesting what is important." Cramer says the vast majority of U.S. media are guilty of this.

He may be overstating things, but certainly we can find much to improve in the reporting and writing most radio and television newscasts. We can do that by becoming expert in the use of our tools – the words. We would not think much of a carpenter who was trying to pound nails with a pipe wrench, nor would we feel much confidence in a doctor who failed to perform necessary tests. As professional journalists, we must become expert in the use of all our tools.

In all news writing – but especially leads – be careful to avoid the overwrought, cliché-soaked sentences epidemic in television news today.

Many great writers intentionally tone down their prose when writing about exotic, lurid, violent or sensational events. Why? Because when the writer resists the temptation to lard his or her copy with overweight adjectives, it allows the impact of the event to connect straight to the listener or reader's heart. Consider this typical lead to a television news story:

"A parent's worst nightmare tonight as a small boy is brutally shot. Our reporter Jesse Aaron has details."

First, let's cast out the cliché "parent's worst nightmare." No one has yet rank-ordered nightmare categories so we don't know which are the worst. Next, let's discard "tonight" because it's a false attempt to infuse our story with breathless immediacy. Finally, we can dump "brutally." Could there be such a thing as a gentle shooting? It would be much more powerful to write something like this:

"Police are searching for a man who shot a five-year-old boy in the arm with a hunting rifle."

In the late 1940's and early 1950's, Jesse Zousmer wrote the hard news that made up the first six or seven minutes of "Edward R. Murrow and the News," a 15-minute radio program launched after World War II. Zousmer was widely considered the best writer in broadcast news. He rarely used adjectives in his short, declarative sentences.

Murrow wrote his own scripts during the war and his clear, authoritative and vivid reporting reassured the nation and made him the most trusted and revered broadcaster of an era. He's considered the father of broadcast journalism.

Murrow and Zousmer's scripts sometimes were so spare they sound today almost like old-fashioned telegrams. Nonetheless, their work offers a lesson in simplicity.

Here's how one Zousmer script began:

> Communist China has rejected the United Nation's peace plan. The communists have offered their own plan. The United States calls it unacceptable.

In broadcast news writing, less often is more.

"The guiding principle in writing news for radio and television is to tell your story as effectively as possible in the fewest number of words," wrote Ed Bliss in his book "Writing News for Broadcast." "Through simplification you improve communication between yourself and the person listening. The listener's mind isn't being cluttered with nonessential information."

Bliss died in 2002 after a long career writing for network news. He is considered one of the finest broadcast news writers ever.

Writing tools

Many writers plod along their entire career without troubling themselves to learn more than a few of the techniques at their disposal. They may use them by accident from time to time, eliciting nods of approval from an editor who recognizes smooth phrasing but is unaware of the tactics that produced it. As professional writers, we need to know what alliteration, parallelism and many other tools are and when they can be employed to make our copy brighter and more memorable.

Spelling

Broadcast journalists tend to worry less about spelling than their print counterparts. People are going to hear my words not read them, radio and TV reporters reason, so why worry? Spell-check programs have made them even less concerned.

But we should double-check our spelling for three reasons:

■ A misspelled word might be pronounced incorrectly.

■ Editors and graphic artists draw on our script for the correct spelling of names, places and things. A recent journalism class of 20 students at California State University Fullerton wrote scripts that involved a character whose last name was Menaldi. Among the variations in finished scripts: Mendali, Mendaldi and Melanie.

■ Pride. Sloppy habits in one area of our work tend to spill over into another.

Here are some writing devices we should know about:

Alliteration – Repetition of initial sound. ("A tale of terror trails the tall tenor")

Allusion – Brief reference to something, often historical or literary, that is commonly known, but not explicitly explained. ("Even Stalin was kind to his dog.")

Analogy – Compares the familiar with the unfamiliar; expands on a simile by comparing several points. ("A computer operates like the human brain – it can take in new information, store it, and retrieve it later.")

Anadiplosis – Repetition of the last word in a sentence or clause near the beginning of the next sentence or clause. ("The Democratic Party stands for justice, and justice is what we will get in the next election.")

Anaphora – Repetition of the same word or phrase at the beginning of successive sentences or clauses. ("America gives me the freedom to learn, America gives me the freedom to worship, America gives me the freedom to work, America gives me the freedom to follow my dreams.")

Antimetabole – Reverses the normal order of words in a line to emphasize contrast. ("Ask not what your country can do for you but what you can do for your country.")

Antithesis – Contrasts two ideas, usually in parallel format, which helps make ideas memorable. ("That's one small step for man, one giant leap for mankind.")

Apophasis – Calling attention to something by negating it. ("We don't really need to say that coal is abundant, cheap, now clean-burning and available.")

Assonance – Likeness of vowel sound in a series of words. ("Some call Cleveland the 'mistake by the lake.'")

Asyndeton – Omitting conjunctions between words. ("After he returned home from the war, he was cheered, lionized, honored.")

Chiasmus – Variation of parallelism that brings together the elements in a way that allows greater contrast. ("The lake fills rapidly but slowly drains." [Straight parallelism would call for the sentence to read: "The lake fills rapidly but drains slowly."])

Climactic order – Building to the most important element. ("The gale blew out the main sail, ripped off a hatch and swept the first mate overboard.")

Consonance – Repetition of the same consonant sound at the end of short word pairs. ("Criss-cross," "Flip-flop," "mish-mash.")

Epanalepsis – Repeated word or phrase at the end of a sentence for emphasis. ("Acid rain ruined this forest; 100,000 trees killed by acid rain.")

Epigram – Terse, witty, pointed statement often with a twist. ("Experience is the name the candidate gives to his bad decisions.")

Exclamation – Sudden outcry.

Hyperbole – Exaggeration; the opposite of understatement. ("The entire street was a moving mass of skateboarders.")

Hyperbaton – Changing the normal word order. ("Forget me not.")

Irony – Deliberate contrast between an expected action or reaction and the actual action or reaction. ("The house was weathered, dirty and small – and Rita, a housecleaner, liked it immediately.")

Metaphor – Compares two different things, which similes and analogies do, but without using "like" or "as." ("Identity thieves are kidnappers of the soul.")

Onomatopoeia – Word whose pronunciation approximates the sound the word makes. ("Buzz," "shrill," "zip.")

Oxymoron – Seemingly contradictory concepts or characteristics written together. ("He said he was proud of his humility.")

Paradox – An apparent contradiction. ("Somehow, they sailed onto dry land.")

Parallelism – Presenting several ideas or options of equal weight in the same format. ("To learn to lead, to learn to follow, to learn to think – these are the objectives of officer training school.")

Personification – Assigning human attributes to animals, insects or things.

("The chocolate did not agree with me.")

Pleonasm – Use of more words than necessary. ("Pick and choose," "well and truly," "part and parcel.")

Polysyndeton – The structural opposite of an asyndeton – all words in the list are preceded by a conjunction, creating a build-up effect. ("They studied and they ran, and they drilled and they tested – that's how it went all day.")

Puns – Plays with multiple meanings of a word. ("Kodak earnings are a picture of losses.")

Rhetorical question – The answer is implied. ("Should parents then demand that school washrooms be cleaned?")

Simile – Comparison of two things using "like" or "as." Used to create vivid imagery and to emphasize what has happened. In his report on the liberation of the Buchenwald prison camp in World War II, Edward R. Murrow described men barely able to greet the Americans. They were so weak, Murrow wrote, that their applause "sounded like the handclapping of babies."

Synecdoche – Metaphor that substitutes a part of something for the entire object. "He lacked cleats (shoes), a number (shirt), and shins (shin guards)."

Understatement – Deliberately reducing the impact of something for effect – the opposite of hyperbole. ("He surveyed the wrecked hull and said 'it could use a little paint.'")

More tools – and how to use them

■ Develop a thought completely and then move on. Doubling back, unless we are foreshadowing, tends to confuse the listeners and viewers. Same rule applies to bites. To the greatest degree possible, introduce a character, use their bite, and move on.

■ Specific is better than general. For example, how old is elderly? Give the age and let the listener/viewer decide. What is blistering heat? Better to give the exact temperature and leave the blistering exaggeration out. When does a chase become "high speed?" Tell listeners and viewers instead what the top speed was – if we're lacking pictures of the actual chase, that fact will enable the listeners and viewers to visualize it and can make the story much more memorable. (I'm still trying to visualize a report in 2004 about a motorcyclist in Minnesota cited by police after aerial surveillance timed him at 200 miles per hour.)

■ Generally speaking, we need to give the listener and viewer the theme sentence – "the reason we are telling you this" – in the first 20 seconds.

■ Write the story with strong supporting facts. Discard weak or insignificant information, but seek out telling details such as a mayor's refusal to use email or an executive's decision to drive an economy car. In television news, merely showing such details is powerful. For example, we could spend many seconds describing an executive as wealthy, successful and socially prominent. But a three-second video clip of the executive's walk-in closet showing two racks of suits and tuxedos, a glass case of neatly rolled ties, and shelves of custom-made dress shirts would "say" all that – without a word from the reporter.

■ Help listeners and viewers find solutions to problems. Guide them to places where they can find more information. Include bites from people who are working on the problem.

■ Accuracy is vital to the carpenter, dentist and seamstress. It's also critical to the journalist.

■ Vary sentence length. For example, a short sentence following a long one serves to emphasize the information presented in the longer sentence. Think of yourself as a composer. If the song kept the same beat throughout, it would sound monotonous. So will our news story.

■ Compound adjectives require a hyphen – in print and in broadcast scripts. Why broadcast? Because it can make a difference in how the passage is read and how the meaning is understood. "A single-passenger airplane" would be read differently on air than "a single passenger airplane." The newsreader would pause between "single" and "passenger" in the non-hyphenated reading to make it clear he or she was talking about one passenger airliner. But "single" and "passenger" would be read in a blended way in the hyphenated version to show that we're talking about an airplane that carries just one passenger.

■ Use strong verbs. Vivid, evocative verbs are the best tools for bringing a script to life.

One important verb to avoid: "continue." Almost always, we can find

Punctuation

Broadcast writing makes great use of punctuation to help guide the newscaster, who may be seeing the copy for the first time when he or she reads it on air.

Good writing has more in common with good music than many news writers realize. Rhythm, flow and cadence are as important to a well-written news story as they are to a song. Yet many writers use the same literary devices over and over, and the same limited punctuation – commas and periods.

But the writer has many more tools to use – each creating different notes in their writing.

Here's how each of our punctuation tools works:

Periods create a sharp break, almost like a staccato ending in music. In countries of the old British Empire, the period at the end of the sentence is called a "full stop," which perhaps better describes the little dot's role in the rhythm of writing than "period."

Commas suggest momentary pause, like the rest sign in music.

Semi-colons call for a slight hesitation; and then a slight change of course in the sentence.

Colons call for a change in tempo. A list may follow, for example, of steps to take: report, write, rewrite.

Dashes suggest a brisk halt, a pause – before proceeding again.

Ellipses... suggest a momentary slowing, perhaps to foreshadow a change in focus.

The listeners and viewer cannot see any of these tools, but they can hear them in the change of voice inflection. Good writers learn how to deploy all the punctuation tools at their command.

a more precise, evocative verb. Was the city council still meeting at broadcast time? Then perhaps we can say they are "plodding through the agenda to the key issue – a proposal to allow teen clubs to serve beer and mixed drinks." Characterize the situation in some way – almost anything is better than "continue."

Another word we often can excise from broadcast copy is the conjunction "that." For example, if we eliminate it from "he said that he was tired," we have made the sentence tighter without losing a shred of meaning.

Sometimes though, we need that, as in "she stressed that the vote was symbolic." If we omit "that" the listener must absorb the entire sentence to make sense of it.

■ Go easy on the adjectives. Let the facts speak for themselves. If you

Storytelling

Since our earliest ancestors first etched drawings and symbols on the walls of caves, we have liked to hear, tell, and read stories. The best news stories employ narrative devices used by storytellers since before the printing press:

Plot

Characterization

Scene setting

Foreshadowing

Action

Dialogue

Dramatization

Conflict

Causation

Myth – The reporter's role often is to dispel them

Metaphor, Simile

Explanation

Twists/surprises

Sequencing – A beginning, middle and end

use vivid verbs and carefully selected facts, vague adjectives become useless anyway. Consider this sentence: "The giant bomber took off for Iraq." How big is "giant"? What was the take-off like?

Better to say: "The eight-engine bomber thundered into the night. Its destination: Iraq."

Avoid the temptation to dust off an adjective to emphasize the obvious. We don't need to add "whopping" in front of "$465 million deficit." But we might want to add a phrase that helps people put that figure into perspective. We could say the deficit is "equal to all the money spent by the city on police services for two years."

■ Avoid pronouns in leads. "It's been described as the biggest... ."

Here's one a producer wrote as a voice-over one summer when ocean sunfish were appearing in big numbers off the Southern California coast: "They're shaped like a dinner plate... can grow up to ten-feet long and weigh up to a ton."

We don't talk to people that way in real life because it's confusing and we shouldn't do it in broadcast for the same reason.

A little re-writing replaced the "they" subject and made the sentence more natural: "Boaters and fishermen are finding dozens of ocean sunfish basking in coastal waters."

■ Be a good observer. On television, the viewers can see the pictures; they depend on us to explain them. In a piece on prison gangs, Los Angeles television reporter Chris Blatchford once narrated over a B-roll of a prison that it was "silent with fear." Everyone can immediately connect with that feeling.

■ A strong story has an emotional core. Find a focus that reaches viewers' and listeners' hearts.

■ Sort things out for the audience. Don't just toss together quotes from people on two sides of a story and expect the audience to sort out the story.

Do the work for them.

■ Build a chronology. It will help sort out causes and effects.

■ Carefully wean the script of any traces of bias. We're neutral observers. As such, copy should avoid characterizations such as "sadly," "hopefully," or any other labels. Give the listeners and viewers the facts and let them decide.

■ It's better to say what something is rather than what it is not. Double negatives, such as "not uncommon" are particularly difficult to process when we hear them. Rather than saying that someone is "not happy" about a particular situation, say instead what he or she is angry about. Rather than saying someone is "no stranger to controversy," (a cliché anyway), it's better to say he "angered people when... ."

Fact checking

After the script is written, one step remains – and most journalists skip this one. That's unfortunate.

Fact check your work. Call your sources back and check one more time on names, spellings, figures, dates, places, events, colors – all the factual elements of your work. It will only take a few minutes and will prevent you from getting calls after the piece has broadcast saying you made a mistake.

Broadcasting is more forgiving of mistakes than print, where the errors are there for all to see. But we owe our fellow citizens our best effort, and that means getting easily verifiable facts right – all the time.

Sometimes errors are repeated so often they begin to be accepted as true. But the World Wide Web has provided a place for more watchdogs of the media. One of them is the non-profit Statistical Assessment Service, which produces the annual "Dubious Data Awards." Some citations in a recent report:

■ "More African-American men are incarcerated than enrolled in college" is an often-reported comparison. A more statistically accurate examination of college-age black men shows 469,000 in college and 180,000 in prison in 2001.

■ Fox News' "O'Reilly Factor" said more than 100,000 children are abducted annually by strangers. The real figure is 3,000 to 5,000.

■ NBC's "Today" show and CNN said we don't know how crop circles are made, thus advancing the belief among some that visitors from other planets are mashing down crops in neat circles. Hoaxers in 1992 showed exactly how the circles are made.

Mistakes and sloppy reporting undermine journalism and the faith we ask our fellow citizens to confer on us. Check your work. Always.

89

Broadcast writer's checklist

■ Who, what, when, where, why and how?

■ Attribution at the beginning of the sentence?

■ Titles before names?

■ Strong Verbs?

■ Active voice? (Or do I want passive voice for a reason?)

■ No mid-sentence clauses?

■ Copy that explains the pictures rather than describes?

■ Vague adjectives replaced with specific descriptions?

■ Vivid similes and metaphors?

■ Copy purged of clichés?

■ Figures rounded off where appropriate?

■ Tight bites that speak to the emotional core of the story?

■ Engaging anchor lead?

■ Anchor tag that neatly closes the story?

■ Use similes and metaphors, especially in radio. Saying what something is like offers listeners imagery that facilitates understanding. But be careful of using "like" when the correct phrasing is "such as." "Like" means something is similar to something else – "the submarine was like a bullet slicing through the water" – while "such as" precedes actual examples – "we'll eat more vegetables at dinner, such as carrots and broccoli."

■ Avoid starting a news story with an unfamiliar name. Listeners will be baffled, even if only momentarily. Prepare the listener for the name by saying first the person's occupation, title or function.

So we would write: "The president of the University of Hawaii filed papers today... ." Our next sentence could be: "Evan Dobelle said he... ."

We can eliminate unnecessary names altogether. For example, if our story is about a body found by the river, we don't need to identify the police officer giving us the information. We can simply say, "police said." Adding the officer's name contributes nothing but adds to information overload by giving the listener more information to process than necessary.

■ Ideally, each sentence should contain just one idea or image.

■ Contractions are used more frequently in broadcast writing than in print. They're easier on the ear.

■ It's acceptable to repeat a key fact in a broadcast script if it needs extra emphasis.

■ Because broadcast news is immediate, listeners and viewers know we may not have all the information – yet. It's important to say what we don't yet know. And it's important to be extremely careful with speculation. In a plane crash, for example, it typically takes the National Transportation Safety Board months of study before it presents its findings. When

American Airlines Flight 587 crashed shortly after takeoff from John F. Kennedy Airport in New York on Nov. 12, 2001, speculation immediately focused on terrorism. But when the NTSB report came out in October 2004, it showed pilot error caused the crash. The co-pilot had worked the rudder back and forth rapidly, trying to get out of wake turbulence created by a Boeing 747 that had departed ahead of it.

■ Finally, refrain from copying source material. We want to create our own work. And it's plagiarism – stealing – to use someone else's words.

Knowing how to use all these tools is essential for every professional reporter, but a command of journalism mechanics is only part of what is required to become a trusted storyteller.

Consider this from Lucille de View, a revered writing coach:

"Love words. Infuse your writing with humanity and truth.

"Our experiences are the ghosts that give us our power to touch readers, listeners and viewers.

"Love the work you do. Take pride and pleasure in it. Work at it. Explore new ways to say old things.

"Celebrate when you pull off the right thought.

"Live fully. Laugh a lot. Don't be afraid to cry.

"Never lose your sense of wonder and the beauty of the human spirit."

Chapter 2.4

Purging clichés, redundancies, and euphemisms

Clichés sap the life out of a story just like a whiff of sewage can ruin a supper party. Unfortunately, broadcast, web and print news writing is soaked with clichés. We have a profusion of raging brushfires, heavy winds and tragic accidents.

It's much better to tell simply and specifically what happened. Tempted to use a cliché? Get a good verb instead. That and a simile or metaphor will bring what you are trying to describe more vividly to life.

"The fire was so hot it melted the windows."

"Besides turning houses into unrecognizable piles of rubble, the hurricane's 160 mile-per-hour winds were powerful enough to propel shafts of straw into telephone poles. When the winds finally diminished, some of the poles looked as if they had been shot with thin arrows."

"The victim's head was pocked with dents where her attacker's hammer had struck."

Good reporters look for those telling details; the rest settle for a cliché. Even when using a specific simile or metaphor, it's easy to fall into the cliché trap. That applies to "arrow straight," "lightning fast," and "whirlwind tours."

If you have heard the phrase before, toss it out and create an original one.

Here are some phrases that long ago grew stale and hackneyed. It is merely a starter list – hundreds more such overused phrases are dumped into news scripts every day.

Clichés are on the left; a simpler word or phrase is on the right.

Purging clichés, redundancies, and euphemisms

Aftermath – following
Against the backdrop – comes as
Area residents – neighbors, people who live here
Around the clock – continuous
Back to the drawing board – start over
Bare minimum – minimum
Bargaining table – negotiated
Behind the wheel – driving
Bid farewell – said goodbye
Bizarre twist – odd
Blanket of snow – snowfall
Bottom line – conclusion
Bracing – getting ready
Broke her/his silence – said
Calls it quits – quits
Calm before the storm – calm
Cautious optimism – hopeful
Chilling effect – discouraged
Choked with emotion – cried
Closely watched – (say why it is important)
Closure – (usually there is no such thing)
Cobble together – put together
Comes as no surprise – expected
Coveted title – title
Cries of protest – protest
Crisis – (is it indeed a crisis or just a problem?)
Critical mass – enough
Crystal clear – clear
Cutting edge – new
Defining moment – when...
Delegate-rich – say how many
Densely wooded area – forest
Doomed to failure – doomed
Drew fire – (passive; usually best to use "attacked" or "fired")
Drop in the bucket – tiny

Dying breed – few remaining

Earmarked – (save this word for cattle references)

Economic crunch – (be specific; factory orders falling, jobless numbers rising...)

Emotional roller coaster – emotional extremes

Epidemic proportions – epidemic

Erupted in violence – broke out

Escaped death – escaped

Faint-hearted – squeamish

Face lift – renovated

Fell on deaf ears – ignored

Few and far between – few

Fled on foot – ran away

Foul play – violence

Gearing up – preparing

Grassroots – started at the bottom

Grief stricken – grieving

Hail of bullets – gunfire

Hammered out – negotiated

Hard line – stubborn, inflexible

Heated debate – angry debate

Heavy – weighed as much as a (brick, bowling ball, anything familiar)

Heightened criticism – growing criticism

Held talks/a meeting – talked, met

High-speed chase – chase

Hit the campaign trail – campaigned

Horrific – (tell the listener/viewer how)

Hotly contested – (show how, give an example)

Hushed courtroom – silent courtroom

In the wake of – following

Jump start – stimulated, ignited

Kick off – began (unless we're writing about a football game)

Laundry list – list

Legend/legendary – (say what our subject accomplished)

Left their mark – (well, what was it?)

Level playing field – fair

Purging clichés, redundancies, and euphemisms

Limped into port – managed to get to port

Lip service – said

Litany – list

Litmus test – (explain what determined the outcome)

Made off with – took

Makeshift – informal (or better yet, describe)

Manicured lawns – neatly trimmed

Media circus – (tell how many reporters were there)

Miraculous escape – (describe how and let the listeners draw their own conclusions)

Mother Nature, Old Man Winter, Jack Frost – (delete unless you can get a bite from them)

Motorists – drivers

New lease on life – (what, the owner didn't renew the old one?)

Only time will tell – we don't know yet

Outpouring of support – (say how much and where it came from)

Naked eye – (ever seen a clothed eye?)

Notified next of kin – told relatives

No relief in sight   we don't know when

(It's) no surprise – (so what is it?)

(he/she was) not alone – (say how many)

Packing x x x-mph winds – generating

Paradigm shift – change

Paved the way – prepared

Play host – host (children may play; we actually will do it)

Pick and choose – (either one, but not both)

Political football – (say why no one wanted to associate with the issue)

Political observers – experts

Poster child – example

Predawn darkness – just before sunrise

Raging brushfire – (ever seen a happy one?)

Rain failing to dampen – despite the rain... .

Raise the bar – boost standards

Ramp up – prepare

Rank and file – union members

Ratchet up – increase

Reign of terror – frightening

Rush to judgment – hurried

Seesaw battle – contested

Skyrocketing – rose

Sped to the scene – rushed

Special – (say how)

Spoke out – spoke

Spread like wildfire – spread quickly

Still at large – not found yet

Strife-torn – (say what the trouble is)

(Country) strongman – dictator

Sweltering, frigid temperatures – (Because temperature is a measure, it cannot be hot or cold. Just give the degrees and the listener will decide if it qualifies as sweltering, frigid or whatever other adjective we have been tempted to use.)

Tempers flared – angered

Third world – (this term arose during the Cold War when the world was divided into three camps – democracies, communist nations and undecided countries. It's more accurate now to just say "poor.")

Threw up their hands – quit

Tip of the iceberg – small part

Under siege – attacked

Uphill battle – (is it a downhill battle for the opponents?)

View with alarm – alarmed

Went missing – disappeared

White stuff – snow

Wide-ranging – (how wide?)

Window of opportunity – chance

Work cut out for him/her – (in a sawmill?)

Worst-case scenario – if everything goes wrong...

Worst nightmare – worst fear

Wreaked havoc – destroyed...

Redundancies

Good writers avoid using extra words. Redundancies are like extra weights in the trunk of a car – they cause it to sag and go slower.

Here are some examples of common redundancies:

Brutal murder – Is there such a thing as a gentle murder?

Complete stranger – Can there be an incomplete stranger? Someone is either a stranger or not.

Controversial issues – By definition, an issue is controversial. No need to use both words.

Future plans – By definition, all plans are future.

In fact – Well, that's what we do in journalism, right?

Nose dive – A dive is head (OK, nose) first. Otherwise, it's a jump.

Of course – So we don't need to say.

Past history – By definition, all history is past.

So-called – "Called" is fine; the "so" adds nothing.

Tragic accident – Just say what happened and let the listener or viewer decide if it's tragic.

Unanswered questions – By definition, a question lacks an answer.

Jargon, technical language and legal pillows

Almost as deadly to a news report as clichés is jargon, the specialized terms used by certain occupations or groups. And as the world gets more complex every day, so does the temptation to lard a story with technical terms, legalese, bureaucratese, and bafflegab.

Among the terms to avoid in news copy: bottom line, conceptualize, feedback, infrastructure, optimize, and parameter. Hundreds more such words and phrases sneak into news stories. Be vigilant. Keep such terms out of your copy.

Police stories offer the greatest temptation for journalists to start talking like cops. Police may say "two male perpetrators fled on foot from the robbery scene after dropping a bag of a controlled substance," but for our story let's say "police say they are searching for two men who ran away after robbing a liquor store and dropping a bag of cocaine."

Avoid the police term "suspect," but if you must use it, remember it applies only to specific, identified individuals. Our liquor store robbers are not "suspects" until police identify them. And victims are taken to hospitals; let the police use "transported."

We must distill legalese to terms ordinary people can understand. A few years ago, two big dogs killed a woman in an apartment complex. A news report said the owner of the dog was charged with "having a mischievous animal that killed a human being." That's probably how the statute reads and how the district attorney described the charge. But we have to simplify that. "Charged with keeping a vicious dog" is accurate and will be understood by our audience.

When police do catch suspected bad guys and put them in jail, they write a report about the violations their police work has uncovered. The district attorney then reads the report and decides whether to file charges. We can write "police say" or "police booked the man on armed robbery charges." We should avoid the temptation to insert "allegedly" or "reportedly," two words a journalist can go an entire career without using. Many journalists use "alleged," "allegedly" and "reportedly," thinking these words provide some sort of protection, a legal pillow of sorts, under their story. They do not and the reporter who thinks so sooner or later will learn a hard lesson in libel from a "suspect's" lawyer.

Finally, when those two men we talked about earlier are arrested for robbery and go to court to be formally charged, let's say that instead of "arraigned," another legal term non-lawyers are apt to confuse.

Euphemisms

These are vague or softened expressions used in place of words that some might consider unduly harsh. And in these ever more politically correct times, the list of euphemisms is growing swiftly.

So we have few poor people these days but we do have many of low income. Some of these low-income people may attempt to get into affordable housing, which is correctly called subsidized. Whether they get their house or not, they never will grow old but instead will evolve into senior citizens. And none of their children will be lazy students but they may have a learning disability.

We want to be sensitive to the groups we are reporting on but not to the extreme of obscuring the true meaning of what we write.

It's all right to call a "rest room" or "comfort station" a toilet.

It's OK to refer to an "account executive" as a salesman or saleswoman.

It's fine to use garbage collector instead of "sanitation engineer."

Vagaries

Give listeners and readers a clear basis for visualizing something. Years ago, hundreds of reports were written and broadcast about some mudslides in Southern California. All described the slides as "massive." Well, how big is "massive?" How much does it take to make something "huge?"

Take the extra reporting step and find out how much mud actually came down. Even if you only can get an estimate – "enough to fill 30 freight cars" – that's better than "massive."

"More than" and "less than" almost always can be replaced with "about." One less word and it's more accurate.

Real people in real conversations rarely use as many hackneyed phrases as journalists do in their scripts or in print. See how many clichés you can find in this one-act play called:

"On Deadline"

(Scene opens in a living room where the telephone is ringing. An answering machine kicks on: Hi – Ethel, Jim, Enrique, Rasheed and Tamiko are not in right now but if you'll leave a message we'll try to get back to you within a fortnight.)

Voice on machine: Jim, this is Ed, your editor. I'm editing your story on the family that was torn apart – by a... pack of wolves?! We're not telling the readers that until the 6th graf! Call me Jimmy.

(Jim enters the room and plops in a chair. His daughter Tamiko walks in.)

Tamiko: Dad – I want to go with Erika and Tanisha to Cozumel for spring break.

Jim: Oh, and how are you going to pay for that?

Tamiko: Well, I have a war chest. (She's wearing a T-shirt with "War" written on it.)

Jim: That's a drop in the bucket compared to what you will need.

Tamiko: But dad, if I don't go it will have a chilling effect on my social standing at school.

Jim: I was bracing for that argument. But it comes against the backdrop of underachievement on your last report card.

Tamiko: You're saying my grades were crummy?

Jim: Yes.

(Phone rings again.)

Tamiko: Are you going to answer it?

Jim: No, it's probably either a telemarketer or an editor.

(Tamiko leaves the room.)

Phone: Jim, this is Ed again. Getting near deadline here and I have another question. In the graf after the one about the calm before the storm but before the one about the high-speed chase, you mention a dying breed. Help me transition all this Jimmy.

(Enter Rasheed.)

Rasheed: Hey pop. I want to buy a motorcycle.

Jim: No motorcycles in this house. They are involved in some horrific accidents. I myself barely escaped death once.

Rasheed: Wasn't that because your bike had bald tires and Mother Nature had just dropped a blanket of the white stuff?

Jim: All I recall is that I made a miraculous escape when a motorist almost ran me down.

(Rasheed shrugs and leaves the room. Enter Ethel.)

Ethel: I'm going to the school meeting tonight to complain about the nomenclature in this documentation.

Jim: You're going to speak out?

Ethel: Yes, I'm going to break my silence.

Jim: Tempers will flare.

Ethel: Maybe, but I think we can launch a grassroots effort.

Jim: What are political observers saying?

Ethel: That it's a closely watched controversial issue. But that it's only fair to have a level playing field, to end the reign of terror before it spreads like wildfire.

Jim: Wait a minute! Isn't it redundant to say an issue is controversial? I think I read something about that in Journalism 101. Anyway, is this thing being viewed with alarm? Could it be a seesaw battle?

Ethel: Yes. We're under siege.

(The phone rings again. Ethel leaves the room; Enrique enters.)

Enrique: Eh, papa, answer the phone?

Jim: No, it's probably a wrong number.

Phone: Jimmy! Ed here. Call me A-S-A-P. I don't understand this reference in your story to the brutal murder.

Purging clichés, redundancies, and euphemisms

Enrique: Can I borrow $10?

Jim: For?

Enrique: Lunch tomorrow. I want to take Tessa out.

Jim: Is she that tall, willowy Samoan girl? The one who was burned in the upper torso in that house fire that was fully involved?

Enrique: I don't think so. She stated her family is from impoverished Guatemala.

Jim: Are they the ones that won the coveted title? Lotto Kings?

Enrique: No, they entered but were doomed to failure. I tried to warn them but it fell on deaf ears.

Jim: Where you going to go for this lunch?

Enrique: Vicencios. It's two-for-one day tomorrow.

Jim: Is that the place near where the brushfire raged?

Enrique: No, it's where that gang of Swedish kids fired a hail of bullets though the windows. They're still at large.

Jim: Can you see the bullet holes with the naked eye?

Enrique: Yeah, and they're the biggest holes in recent memory. It was heavy man.

Jim: Heavy? How heavy? Well be careful son, you never know when things may erupt in violence again.

Enrique: That's what area residents are saying. Only time will tell.

(The phone rings again as Enrique walks out of the room, pausing to glance at the phone and then his father. A clearly agitated Rasheed bursts into the room again. He too ignores the phone.)

Rasheed: Someone turn on a radio or television. I've been outside for a few minutes and out of touch with what's happening.

Phone: James!!! I know you're there. Pick up the phone. Jimmy? We're right on deadline.

(Rasheed turns on a small radio and inserts the earpiece. He listens intently for a moment.)

Jim: Son, what's the very latest?

Rasheed (his back to the window, facing his father): Well as you can see behind me down there at the harbor, the legendary SS Disney has limped into port after someone threw a karaoke machine overboard and it heavily damaged a propeller.

Jim: Any suspects?

Rasheed: No but police have thrown up a perimeter around the area and are warning area residents to keep their karaoke machines out of sight until this senseless crime is solved. Back to you, Dad.

Jim: All right Rasheed. Thank you for that.

(Rasheed nods and continues listening, his hand holding the earpiece in place.)

Jim: Time I think for me to tune in to the evening news. I've got to gear up for another day in the newsroom tomorrow. But I fear there is no relief in sight from... Ed.

(Phone rings.)

Phone: It's Ed again. We're holding your story.

Chapter 2.5

Writing for radio

Most textbooks treat writing for radio and writing for television as interchangeable. Yes, the basic principles are the same. But radio lacks pictures that can carry a weak script.

In radio, good writing is essential.

Here are some tips from Robert Sims, former news director of KNX radio in Los Angeles and one of the most respected radio journalists in the nation:

The writing should be simple and clear; avoid long convoluted sentences.

■ Change the pattern of sentence length. Lots of too-short sentences can be just as deadly as the over-long sentence.

Use present tense whenever feasible. "He defends his policy" rather than "he defended his policy."

Eliminate needless detail but make sure to retain the essential facts.

Condense long titles.

■ Most quotes sound better when carefully and accurately paraphrased. Avoid using "quote" and "unquote."

Determine when precise attribution is important; and, on the other hand, when attribution is not even needed. For example, we don't have to attribute the fact that a building is burning to firefighters.

Be careful of gee-whiz writing, characterized by such phrases as "the first of it's kind."

Avoid unnecessary adverbs – "flatly denied," "sharply rebuked," "Bitterly denounced."

Read aloud what you have written. Sometimes what may look fine on paper sounds awkward when verbalized.

■ On an ongoing story, keep freshening the lead. Although the original focus of the World Trade Center attacks was on the aircraft crashing into the buildings, the emphasis then changed to the fires, then to the building collapses, then to the rescue efforts.

■ It's all right in broadcast news writing to use sentence fragments and begin sentences with "and." "And that's not all the president said."

■ Be careful how lines of copy end. Although professional broadcasters learn to "see ahead," it still can cause the newscaster to pause at the wrong place if "bird" is at the end of one line and "feeder" is on the next line. Hyphenating such words will keep them on the same line.

■ Watch out for too many "he's" and "she's" in radio broadcast copy after identifying them at the beginning of the story. In a television news story, we typically see the subject several times. But the radio listener has no such assistance and often is distracted while listening. Repeat the person's name – it serves as a reminder to the listener.

Radio terminology

Actuality – Recording of quotes on tape. Also called a sound bite or cut.

Ambient sound – Sound from the news scene – dogs barking, a crowd cheering. Same as nat (natural) sound in television.

Back announce – Identify the person speaking after an actuality. ("That was Angela Yau.")

Button – A short piece of music used in a news magazine to signal movement from one story to another.

Cue – Signal to begin. May come from announcer, piece of music, or other indicator.

Cutaway – Point at which newscast can cut to other programming.

Evergreen – Feature story that can be held for use on a slow news day.

Incue/outcue – Words that begin/end an actuality.

Lockout – Reporter's close ("In Fullerton, I'm Elliot Blair Smith").

Open with sound – Opening the report with either an actuality or ambient sound.

Sounder – Short musical opening to a newscast.

Upcut – Actuality that finishes at a point when the person's vocal inflection suggests he or she is about to say something else. Avoid using these, but if you must, the reporter must finish the speaker's thought by writing something that connects the last word of the actuality with what is to follow.

Voicer – Story with reporter's voice only.

(radio script sheet)

Slug:	**Date:**
Writer:	**Producer:**
Duration:	**Anchor:**

News copy is written here

Chapter 2.6

Writing for the web

Writing for the web is both a venture to journalism's new frontier and a return to the earliest days of electric journalism.

The web is so new as a medium that definitive guidelines on how to write for online reading and viewing still are evolving. And yet, what we do know fairly conclusively is that web viewers overwhelmingly tend to be scanners, looking for keywords, sub heads, bullet points, lists and other tools that will allow them to get quickly into the information before them.

To many web-writing researchers, that means a return of the old inverted pyramid developed for the telegraph era so the most important facts would be presented first and the remaining information in descending order of significance.

Other storytelling approaches can work on the web, but certainly for breaking news, speed and conciseness are valued.

Here are some web-writing basics for breaking and spot news stories:

■ Get the essence of the story into the lead, which often doubles as the headline. Our success in telling viewers at a glance what our story is about will determine whether viewers keep reading or click away.

■ Begin paragraphs with a clear topic sentence, rather than an anecdotal, question or scene-setter one.

■ Keep all sentences and paragraphs short. Simple declarative sentences free of mid-sentence clauses are best.

■ Use bulleted lists to break out and condense information.

■ Consider boldfacing the most important phrases in each paragraph. This will serve the viewer who is scanning.

■ If you have more than one source, strive to contain quotes and attributable information for each of them in one paragraph. This also helps the fast-moving scanner-viewer who is reluctant to scroll back if they get to a second reference or quote and cannot remember the first reference.

Web site reader retention falls off sharply below what appears on the screen; that is, for text requiring scrolling. Keep your stories short and focused. Viewers can get more in the paper, or later on the site.

Below is a piece written specifically for the web. Note that the headline doubles as the lead, and key elements are set in bold type so the very busy viewer can skim even faster. Bullet points also help the viewer zip through the piece. For the viewer slightly less time-challenged, the bold-facing and bullet points tend to reinforce important material. Finally, note the links to more information, which web users expect.

The business world's most enduring star will visit Orange County on Monday with a new bundle of messages he says will help make every company run better.

Tom Peters will lead an all-day **seminar** called "Reinventing the Rules for the Brand-New Workplace" at the **Anaheim Marriott Hotel.**

Peters says some of the **new success rules** are:

* **Put a distinctive brand** on your work, your product or your service.

* **Actively forget the old ideas** that are holding you and your organization back.

* **Go from customer satisfaction to customer success** by providing solid benefits to the bottom line.

Moreover, Peters says today's workers need to "turn themselves into one-person brands. Act like a professional services firm."

Peters also champions what he calls **"Wow! Projects,"** things that shake up the old ways. Tomorrow's successful organizations will appreciate such efforts, he says.

Peters has built a career on shaking up the old ways of doing business although he says today he had "no idea" what he was doing when he wrote "In Search of Excellence."

Yet if music stars would stay ahead of trends the way Peters does, the music scene still would be dominated by Lionel Ritchie, Blondie and Kim Carnes. Those singers were among the biggest hit makers in 1981, the year Peters and Robert Waterman Jr. published "In Search of Excellence."

Since then, Peters has been a human dynamo. He has published nine more books, created 22 videotapes and speaks or leads about 100 seminars a year. In his spare time, he runs a farm in Vermont.

For more information on Peters' program Monday in Anaheim, go online to **www.lessonsinleadership.com** or call **1-800/873-3451.**

Chapter 2.7

Writing safely and avoiding lawsuits

It's probably fitting that the last chapter of this book be devoted to legal considerations of broadcast news writing. Lawyers always get the last word, right?

The station's attorney certainly should get the final read on any story that may have legal ramifications.

A sure way to ruin a journalism career is to libel or slander someone. Even defending a lawsuit can cost a broadcast company tens of thousands of dollars. A protracted legal battle easily can run into the hundreds of thousands of dollars. That could break a station's finances and indelibly tarnish your career, even if you win.

It's imperative to know the fundamentals of laws governing what can and cannot be said and written, not just so we avoid getting sued, but also because we do not want to sully someone's reputation unfairly.

First of all, know that libel refers to statements in print; slander to spoken statements. But it's not that simple. A broadcast story can fall under the laws of libel because it is derived from a written script.

Know the basics of the laws on libel and slander so you will know when you get near a danger zone and need to consult the station's lawyer.

Here are the legal concepts every reporter must know from day one on the job:

Fairness

This refers to balance. If we are preparing a report on criticism of an official, company or organization, we must make a good-faith effort to give that person or entity a chance to respond. This does not refer to critical reviews of movies, books and plays.

Defamation

A person's reputation can be damaged by what is spoken or printed.

If it is spoken, such as in a live report, the defamation may fall under slander laws. However, courts generally have ruled that when a broadcast is disseminated to a mass audience from a written script, it falls under libel statutes.

Identification does not have to be by name. It can be by description, occupation, or association.

The person suing must prove some degree of fault, malice, negligence or reckless disregard for the truth.

The defense

Truth – Truth is an important ally to the journalist being sued. You may believe your information to be solid, but can it be proven?

Privilege – Laws vary from state to state, but generally this means you are safe to quote from to documents, testimony, and comments made in official proceedings. Comments in a hallway outside court do not fall under the privilege statute.

Fair comment – News stories on the actions of people and institutions affecting the public are safe if they have a basis in truth and are not done maliciously. Be careful – Fair Comment protection does not extend to false and defamatory statements.

Note also the use of the term "allegedly" offers almost no legal protection. Be careful of what is reported beyond that a crime has been committed and someone is being held for questioning. And remember that the fact that police are questioning someone does not necessarily mean that person is a "suspect."

Privacy: Another danger zone for reporters

False light involves portrayals that distort a person's reputation. Penthouse magazine was sued successfully some years ago for a fictional story whose character resembled the woman who was Miss Wyoming at the time.

Public disclosure of private facts. A man who knocked a gun from the hand of a person attempting to shoot then-President Ford was identified in news accounts as a being a familiar figure in the San Francisco homosexual community. He was in fact a homosexual but had not informed his mother of that fact. The network settled the case out of court.

Trespassing or intrusion refers to the act of intruding, either physically or with a camera. A person's home is considered to be more private than an office. Journalists can be guilty of intrusion even if no information is broadcast or published.

Some years ago, a station that is now poorer lost a court judgment after it broadcast tape of a hefty woman sitting on her porch as part of a piece on obesity and lack of exercise. The woman was completely unaware she was being photographed from afar.

Privacy laws also protect people from being in the news forever. For example, a television station broadcast pictures of child involved in a car accident on the day of the incident. That was OK. Two years later, the station pulled the tape out of its archives and used it in a story about car crashes. The child's parents successfully sued the station for invasion of privacy, arguing their child no longer was "in the news."

Shield laws: Protection differs state to state

Promising confidentiality to a source can be treacherous because of many gray areas in the laws. Before you offer confidentiality, and especially before you broadcast information obtained that way, be sure to consult your executive producer or news director.

When in doubt on any legal matter, consult with your executive producer or news director, whose job it is to know how to handle basic legal problems. For a journalist, legal dilemmas are situations where it is better to be safe than sorry.

Epilogue

Becoming a better writer all the time

Airline pilots, doctors, lawyers and other professionals must constantly upgrade their knowledge or risk quickly becoming incompetent. While many journalists insist they fall into the "professional" category, few make an every-day effort to improve their skills.

Many television journalists learn how to work with their photographer to get the shots they need; they learn how to elicit decent bites from their interview; they learn how to write adequately enough to stitch a package together. But they rarely, if ever, attend journalism conferences or writers workshops and then eventually they become anchors and don't write much anymore anyway.

That's a shame. And it's why much of what passes for news on television is so poorly done.

We owe our fellow citizens more.

Athletes and musicians must work hard to stay in top condition so they can perform at their best. They strive to be better today than yesterday, better tomorrow than today.

We should do the same.

As my father once said: "If you're not improving, then you really are falling behind."

Finally, it's worth remembering why we do this – chasing stories every day, covering people's tragedies, failings and triumphs. Fred Rogers (Mr. Rogers) once said of public broadcasting that it "is at its best when it listens to the heartbeat of a nation and is its quiet servant."

That ought to apply to commercial television newscasts as well.

Acknowledgements

How (and why) this book came about

Some years ago, my mother was watching one of those awards shows on television where the winners clutch their trophy and thank a long list of people for their achievement.

"Just once," my mom said, "I'd like to hear someone on those shows get up and say, "I did it all myself.' "

She was joking – no one wins an Academy Award, Grammy, Emmy or any other award by themselves. At a minimum, a cast of coaches and mentors deserve applause.

And so it is with a book, especially one that purports to teach. My thank-you list includes Joe Kraus, Kent Prince, Bill Crider, Barney Calame, Steve Sansweet, Roy Harris, Bill Blundell, Fred Muir, Bruce Horovitz, Lucille De View, Pete Weitzner and especially, Sister Mary Anderson.

To all of them, I owe a debt I never can repay. They shared their knowledge and inspiration. Any errors, omissions and oversights though are entirely mine.

Print reporters sometimes think of broadcast reporters as dilettantes, more interested in their appearance and their voice than in real news. But the broadcast reporter must produce the clearest of all writing because the listener and viewer get just one pass at the story. The reader can try again to make sense of muddled passage.

I got an early lesson in that as a young writer for the Associated Press. In traffic one day, I listened as the announcer on the radio read my stories just as I had written and transmitted them a few hours earlier. I amused myself wondering if my fellow drivers crawling along during the morning rush and listening to the same station realized the writer of the news they were hearing was me, the guy in the maroon car. But that thought was

Acknowledgements

interrupted as the announcer stumbled a few times while reading my last item. Then when he finished, he said – on the air – "Man, I didn't know what that one was about."

Thanks to my mentors at the AP, that didn't happen again.

In the day-to-day crush of delivering the news, it's easy to overlook that this is the most intriguing, challenging time ever to be a journalist. The old media – newspapers, magazines, radio and television – are converging and a new online medium is being born. We journalists not only get to practice our craft at a pivotal time in history but we also are lucky enough to be pioneers on journalism's new frontier.

Yet while the media change, the demands of clear writing remain the same. The world gets more complex every day and our fellow citizens trust us to sort it out for them. It's to that effort that this book is addressed.

Index

Index

Other journalism titles from Marion Street Press, Inc.